A685

Pelican Books
Who's Watching You?

D0232911

Crispin Aubrey was born in 1946 and has been a journalist since leaving university. After training on a local newspaper in Winchester, he worked for a film trade weekly and, for six years, on London's *Time Out* magazine, writing about social and environmental issues. Among his current interests is a project investigating the problems of alternative and radical publications, a subject on which he writes a monthly column in the *Guardian*.

He is married with three children and lives in Somerset.

Crispin Aubrey

WHO'S WATCHING YOU?

Penguin Books

Penguin Books Ltd, Harmondsworth, Middlesex, England
Penguin Books, 625 Madison Avenue, New York, New York 10022, U.S.A.
Penguin Books Australia Ltd, Ringwood, Victoria, Australia
Penguin Books Canada Ltd, 2801 John Street, Markham,
Ontario, Canada L3R 1B4
Penguin Books (N.Z.) Ltd, 182–190 Wairau Road, Auckland 10, New Zealand

First published 1981
Reprinted 1981

Copyright © Crispin Aubrey, 1981
All rights reserved

Made and printed in Great Britain by
Richard Clay (The Chaucer Press) Ltd, Bungay, Suffolk
Set in Monotype Ehrhardt

To the ABC Campaign

Contents

Preface

This book is not intended as a detailed guide to the organization, techniques and political background of the British security system. But I hope it provides a readable introduction to the subject, based in part on my own experience over almost two years. To assist the reader I have included a number of references in the text to newspaper articles, government reports and so on. Anyone who wants to read more about the activities described should also select from the Bibliography at the end. However I have found most useful, particularly in the research for Chapter 1, Tony Bunyan's *The Political Police in Britain* (see Bibliography) – still the best general work on the subject.

Throughout the book frequent reference will be found to 'the secret agencies', 'the security services' and similar general descriptions of the British organizations of national security. These are meant to be no more than that, and only when a particular organization is mentioned by name, for instance the Special Branch or MI6, is a specific reference to that body intended.

I should like to thank all those who have contributed ideas and comments on the manuscript, as well as Judy Groves, Steve Pinder, Irene Campbell, Jane Rackham and especially Sue Aubrey, who tolerated its gestation. I am also indebted to the organization State Research for use of its facilities.

Introduction

It's all too easy for politicians and experts to pontificate on the weaknesses, or the vital necessity, of the British state security system. For the most part they haven't experienced its powerful presence at first hand. I have.

In 1977 I, and fellow journalist Duncan Campbell, achieved the doubtful notoriety of being the first British reporters to be accused of what amounted to spying. Together with John Berry, a former Corporal who had worked on the initial analysis of intercepted radio signals, we were charged under Section 1 of the Official Secrets Act, normally reserved for foreign spies. Eventually, our case attained a political and legal significance which provided the impetus for writing this book.

The birth of this unique occurrence was a conversation between the three of us at John Berry's Muswell Hill flat in February 1977, of which I made a tape-recording. When we emerged from that interview we were all arrested by the Special Branch, Britain's secret police, and the record of our discussion seized. But though for me that was a shock I am unlikely to forget, to the secret agencies of the state it was a calculated decision. By methods of surveillance which I shall explain in more detail later, they knew we were there and they knew what we were talking about.

In fact the origins of what became known as the 'ABC' case, after the initials of our surnames, can be found well before that eventful evening – in the controversial decision by the Labour government of the time (November 1976) to deport two American writers, Philip Agee and Mark Hosenball. Agee was an ex-CIA agent who had taken the unusual step of writing about his experiences, Hosenball was a staff writer on *Time Out*, a London weekly news and entertainment magazine with a reputation for digging up embarrassing scandals. Both men were said to have threatened the British national security by their actions, although no concrete evidence for this was ever provided. Furthermore, they were given no proper opportunity to contest the allegations. As American citizens they could be thrown out of this country – and they were.

But at the time of our arrest the argument and protest about those deportations was still in full swing, and Duncan Campbell, myself and John Berry were all in different ways concerned. I was then a reporter for *Time Out* magazine. I had also worked at the next desk to Mark Hosenball, and became closely involved in the battle against his and Philip Agee's treatment. Duncan Campbell was an investigative journalist who among other things had written an article with Hosenball about Signals Intelligence, this country's method of international intelligence-gathering by technological means as opposed to human spying. The article was considered one possible reason for Hosenball's deportation. John Berry had in turn worked for Signals Intelligence – and was motivated to talk about his experience by his anger at the deportations.

The combination of the three of us, against the background of an increasing outcry over the Agee–Hosenball case, was one which the security authorities felt unable to ignore. Agee and Hosenball had asked questions, probed, exposed. Now we were apparently about to do the same. We had to be stopped.

Those who tried to stop us ranged from the faceless officials at Government Communications Headquarters in Cheltenham, the centre of British Signals Intelligence, to the officers of the Special Branch, who did the overt work of interviews and arrests – and at least had names. In the shadows were both MI6, the overseas spying network, and MI5, its domestic counterpart. In different ways they all contributed to the decision made by the government's legal adviser, Attorney-General Sam Silkin, to continue with our prosecution.

During the twenty-one months' course of the ABC case the full weight of the machinery of national security descended on the three of us. Dozens of people were interviewed, their homes raided, their personal property seized and their activities watched. Thousands of pounds of public money were spent on investigations, and we were charged eventually under the most oppressive section of the Official Secrets Act.

At our trial, a long list of retired servicemen, technical experts, even a schoolboy and his form master were dragged out of obscurity to testify to our iniquity. There were witnesses without names, proceedings behind closed doors, a jury vetted in advance for its 'loyalty' – all manner of pressures to load the dice in favour of the state. We spent weeks sitting in the Old Bailey, months consulting with solicitors in order to counter the accusation that we had endangered the safety of the nation. Our personal lives were totally disrupted, and all as a result of a single conversation.

In the end the attempt failed. Through a combination of convincing arguments in court and persistent campaigning both by members of the public and by the press, we were able to walk out of the Old Bailey with only the mildest of sentences. The prosecution case was in tatters, official secrecy discredited, the security services, at least temporarily, rebuffed. So why then had the ABC case been taken to such a height of spying paranoia from which it could only tumble?

To answer that question is one of the purposes of this book. But I shall also take a much broader look at the secret agencies of surveillance which exist in Britain today – their methods, their targets and their uniquely privileged position outside the system of democratic accountability through parliament. So far they have only names and initials, but by the end I hope they will acquire flesh, if not blood.

The existence of these organizations is of course not new – there have been state spies ever since governments were formed – nor is Britain unique in having created the superstructure of a potential police state. Around the world, from Iran's now disbanded Savak to South Africa's Bureau of State Security to the Soviet Union's KGB, the well-publicized horrors of torture and imprisonment of dissidents in which such powerful bodies indulge may make some of the incidents described in these pages pall by comparison. But whereas in dictatorships and totalitarian regimes the job of the secret services is to maintain that government in power, their task in a democracy is seen as the defence of individual freedoms – freedom of speech, acquaintance, political dissent.

The most common justification for the activities of the various British secret services is in fact the protection of our 'national security'. This is a phrase which will recur repeatedly in these pages, though it is rarely defined. It is one of those concepts which echoes through the nation's subconscious, tumbles from the lips of politicians and is intended to close the ranks of the patriotic and loyal. If the national security is at risk, runs the unspoken argument, then something drastic must be done. As Lord Denning, one of the most influential judges in Britain, put it during a hearing over the case of deported journalist Mark Hosenball: 'When the state is in danger, our own cherished freedoms, and even the rules of natural justice, have to take second place.'

To many people, a threat to the national security means spying, and historically the secret services have most often received publicity over threats of espionage, especially in wartime. However, the interpretation of 'national security' has changed considerably since the last war. Then, a whole panoply of restrictions – from censorship to internment – was introduced in the face of what most people accepted to be a common enemy, the Germans and their allies. Their sons and daughters may have lost their lives in their thousands, their own homes may have been demolished in the Blitz. But with the imminent possibility that the Nazis might invade, 'our own cherished freedoms' were seen to be directly at stake.

After the war, the 'common enemy' shifted its ground. It was now the countries of the Communist bloc, most immediately the line of new socialist states bordering on Western Europe. The Berlin Wall, with its barbed wire, searchlights and armed guards, symbolized the closed society from which no one could escape. The fear that if the Wall was 'breached' it would mean the enslavement of Europe's democratic nations was fuelled by Western military strategists, who justified their own expenditure on deadly nuclear weapons.

Until recently, it appeared that this Cold War ideology had

receded with the achievement of a crude balance of power between NATO and the Warsaw Pact. Reaction to the presence of Soviet troops in Afghanistan disproved this, as did the election of a strongly anti-socialist Conservative government in Britain. But it is also true that over the past decade or so the defenders of national security have shifted their ground once more. The common enemy is no longer seen (in peacetime) as only concentrated abroad, but also here at home – in the factories, in the streets, in the organizations of protest.

It is of course a simplification to say that the 'enemy within' is something that has been suddenly discovered in the latter half of the twentieth century. It was there in the early 1800s when writers of radical literature were gaoled for sowing the printed seeds of discontent. (The secret service is said to have its origins in the fears of the growing power of literacy.) It was there in the 1920s when millions of people went on strike for better wages. And it has been revived whenever large numbers of people have organized dissent. It was no coincidence when, during our eventual trial, the judge reminded the court that the Official Secrets Act was not just about spies but also the 'internal enemy'.

There have also been some grim justifications for action against this internal enemy. The bombing of a Birmingham pub in 1974, when twenty-one people were killed, was followed by the introduction of the Prevention of Terrorism Act, which allows a suspect to be held for up to seven days without charge. Many people in no way connected with the IRA have since been caught under its provisions and ordered to leave the country, and the threat of terrorism, whether inspired by the Irish conflict or those elsewhere, has come to form a constant backcloth to the work of the security agencies.

But at the same time, those agencies have increased their surveillance of a wide range of legitimate political activity. In particular the Communist Party, the 'reds under the bed' of popular mythology, has achieved the status of a major threat to the national security. Membership of the Party is still a potential handicap in many jobs, yet compared to those of other European countries the British organization is tiny.

And from the Communists the net has literally expanded. As

we shall see, the agencies of national security have, at one time or another, been concerned with such activities as a group of workers who occupied a factory threatened with closure, a man who asked questions about what would happen in the event of a nuclear disaster, and some mothers who protested at the closure of a nursery for their children. In the process, millions of people have been placed on file and subjected to a wide range of surveillance techniques without ever having committed any crime which would be recognizable in a court of law. But for the security authorities those files provide a daily confirmation that their work in peacetime is not in vain.

Those seen to threaten the national security are in turn labelled 'subversive', as Duncan Campbell was during our own case, and through official definitions of this sinister-sounding word it is possible to see how the philosophy of national security has developed. Eighteen years ago, a subversive was described by Lord Denning again as someone 'who would contemplate the overthrow of government by unlawful means'. By 1975, a Home Office Minister, Lord Harris, announced that subversive activities now included those which are intended to 'undermine or overthrow parliamentary democracy by political, industrial or violent means' – no mention this time of breaking the law. Three years later, Home Secretary Merlyn Rees said in parliament that the Special Branch used its powers to 'collect information on people I think are causing a problem for the state'. The shift from revolutionaries to someone who creates discomfort in high places could hardly have been more clearly spelled out.

But it's not only this broadening of the target area of the secret watchers which has caused increasing concern among civil libertarians. The last twenty years have also seen a steady expansion of the security services in terms of their manpower – the Special Branch by six times – their expenditure and their ability to use that money on the most sophisticated techniques of mass surveillance. Electronic listening devices, cameras and the computer have all been developed by the agencies of national security to an extent scarcely dreamed of when they were first created, and often technically in advance of their use in other fields.

To those who defend the activities of the secret agencies, these developments are seen as an acceptable risk. In order to catch the few real subversives, they argue, it is necessary to monitor the activities of thousands of people. In turn, the organizations of political protest have themselves become so fragmented and diverse that it is no longer possible to easily identify the 'enemies of the state'. A continuum is created which starts with urban guerrillas and ends with student protesters. 'We all both want the secret police and hate having them', as David Wood, the political editor of *The Times*, wrote in 1971. 'But it is a necessary evil, and the thought of it is better forgotten or wished away if we are not to be hypocrites.'

By ignoring them, however, we must inevitably overlook two essential elements of their existence. The first is that they are fundamentally defenders of the status quo – the most conservative elements in our society – and that their 'enemies' are those who, for whatever reason, wish to change the political and social system. It will be noticeable during this account that their targets are almost invariably on the left rather than the right of the political spectrum. And the second is that our acquiescence in their work adds to the already powerful veil of secrecy which covers their operations.

Secrecy is not an indivisible concept. It is something which all of us would wish to cover some area of our personal lives. But is it acceptable that organizations with such power should remain, as the secret services do, so independent that not only the general public but the MPs we elect, and even the Ministers who nominally oversee their activities, are excluded from both knowledge and control? As a result, the country's leading politicians are able to pronounce, as they have done, that the security system is neither concerned with anyone's political views, nor does it cross the boundary from legal to illegal action. As we shall see, these statements are of doubtful veracity.

The dangers of this independence have been well summarized by an intelligence man himself, John Bruce Lockhart, during a lecture to the Royal United Services Institute in 1973. The security services can provide false information to governments, he said, in order to protect their own vested interests, or because that is what they think their political masters would like to hear, or simply to cover their own incompetence. In the process, they can develop their own political policies and, by extension, their own conspiracies. They can also involve a government in embarrassing and dangerous operations the risks of which have never been clearly spelled out to the politicians. And, he might have added, they can involve themselves in disasters such as the ABC case.

That, then, is the context in which my own experience of the security services must be seen. I have not written a blow-by-blow account of the ABC case, and many small details have been omitted. Instead, the case has been used to illustrate the way in which the power of national security can be abused. By looking in turn at the various pressures which contributed to our prosecution, from the development of investigative journalism to the fear of 'whistleblowers', I have tried to show how other people can be, and have been, affected, and to isolate the most important issues which emerged. (For readers who may wish to remind themselves of the basic chronology of the ABC case, an appendix of important dates is included.)

One important element of the ABC case needs explaining at the start – the Official Secrets Act under which we were charged. This law remains, at the time of writing at least, both a powerful deterrent against investigation of the security services and a threat to those on the inside who might want to reveal their concern. But though its pervasive effect will be mentioned frequently, this is not primarily a book about the Act and its long history, uses and legal ramifications, and a number of books are mentioned in the Bibliography which adequately cover this area.

Passed through parliament almost seventy years ago, at the time of a German spy scare, the Official Secrets Act prohibits any unofficial disclosure of information about the workings of central government. Both the suppliers and the receivers of such information, however trivial, are liable to prosecution under this heading, which is known as Section 2, and face up to two years in prison. Under its other main heading, Section 1, normally called the 'spying' clause, all disclosure of information which 'might be, directly or indirectly, useful to an enemy' is similarly prohibited. The penalty for breaking this is up to fourteen years in gaol. The Act therefore drastically limits the amount of information available to inform public debate, leaving a decision on disclosure entirely up to the decision-makers and their advisers. Its breadth can be judged from a comment by a former head of MI5, Sir Martin Furnival-Jones, who said in evidence to a government committee: 'It is an official secret if it's in an official file.'

Historically, the law has been used against both admitted spies and journalists, as well as numerous government officials, though our case was the first in which journalists were accused of being spies. It has also been the subject of continuous political debate ever since the reform of Section 2 was first suggested by an official committee of inquiry in 1972. So far, those reforms, however timid, have not yet reached the statute book, one reason being the pressure of the security system (originally responsible for pushing the Act through in the first place) to introduce even tougher sanctions in the areas of defence, intelligence and the police.

Partly because of the limitation on information encouraged by the Official Secrets Act, I have depended to a large extent on the experiences of those who have, for one reason or another, been at the receiving end of the secret state. Whether those experiences are aberrations or whether, as I believe, they represent only the tip of a much larger iceberg, I shall leave to the reader to decide. But he or she must also accept that in some cases individuals have preferred to remain anonymous.

At the same time, there are a number of examples in this book from the United States, where the differing laws and traditions have allowed much more to emerge about the operations of the secret agencies. But it is also true that America provides an important guide to what might already be happening here, or may happen in the future. After all, the security services of the United States not only originated in Britain but work in close cooperation with their British counterparts.

Finally, I should apologize to those readers who might expect it, that there is very little violence in this account. I am not concerned here with the cosh or the rubber bullet but with the policing of the mind. It is often said that the British people have established the right to criticize, protest and dissent. We do not have to wait until the occasional opportunity for placing a piece of paper in a ballot box to do that. However, it is precisely those rights which, in the name of national security, are under attack. If we cannot make a phone call, attend a public meeting or get involved in a trade union without fear of surveillance, where do those freedoms lie? Even talking, as I found to my own cost, can be construed as a threat to the state.

Meanwhile, the security services remain invisible and un-accountable, surrounded by a mystique of dark glasses and turned-up collars. As I write this, hunched over a typewriter, the organizations of national security, hunched over their desks, are making daily judgements as to who will be their targets. Cabinet Ministers may claim this as their responsibility. The reality is that they do not have that control, and have failed to try to obtain it.

The Snatch: 18 February 1977

The rain was falling steadily as my car drew up outside the Muswell Hill terrace. It was half an hour later than I'd arranged for the interview, and I hurriedly gathered together my canvas bag and tape-recorder and dashed across the road. By one of those odd coincidences that the police can interpret as a conspiracy, Duncan Campbell arrived at exactly the same time, having come by tube.

Inside, ex-Corporal John Berry was waiting for us with a welcoming bottle of Italian wine. For several hours, in a relaxed and often chatty atmosphere, he spoke about his experience in Signals Intelligence, Britain's secretive electronic eavesdropping network, his reasons for deciding to talk about it after seven years in civilian life and his increasing disillusionment with the work.[1] We had come prepared for an interesting journalistic encounter and my tape-recorder spun round silently, recording every word.

Just after 10 p.m. we emerged into the cold February gloom. For a moment, Duncan and I stood by my car discussing whether I could give him a lift. Then a group of men appeared dramatically from the darkness. 'We are police officers,' one of them said. 'We have reason to believe that offences have been committed under the Official Secrets Act.' As we later discovered, they were members of the Special Branch.

It was seconds before my stunned brain realized what had happened. But I was brought up sharp by the sound of running feet clattering eerily across the road to the house, the signal for the arrest of our recent contact. My heart beat faster as a Detective Inspector grabbed my canvas bag, quickly discovered the tape-recorder and hustled me towards a waiting Hillman car.

1. What John Berry told us about his experience is described in Chapters 4 and 5.

I asked naively whether I had in fact been arrested. The answer was coldly in the affirmative.

It proved a long drive to Muswell Hill police station, though a local would have taken only a few minutes. But the Special Branch, who had clearly been given an inadequate and hasty briefing, got lost. After a meandering drive round the outskirts of Alexandra Park, the driver stopped, consulted a map and turned round.

When we finally arrived, the Inspector shadowed me into the bare reception room of the station. The contents of my pockets and bag were emptied on to a wooden table – diary, keys, handkerchief, cigarettes, wallet, press cuttings, notebook and the all-important tape-recorder. The black plastic box looked absurdly innocent, but the contents of its two cassettes were soon to set the alarm bells of national security ringing loud.

Having listed my property in a record book, the station Sergeant ushered me into a cell, and the solid metal door banged shut with a hollow boom. Inside, I found a narrow blanketless bed, a small high window at one end and a notice which told me I could see a solicitor if it didn't interfere with further inquiries. I shivered with nervousness.

It seemed an age before Duncan Campbell and John Berry joined me in the adjacent cells. As it turned out, they'd had an even longer journey, one Special Branch driver having to summons a passing taxi to show him the way. It was something to laugh at anyway. As midnight passed, I began to wonder when we would be let out. Surely they couldn't keep us here overnight? A drunken man was brought into the fourth cell in the row, his boozy shouts echoing down the corridor. Apart from that, silence.

I pressed a bell in the wall, a policeman peered through the spy-hole and I asked whether I could make a phone call. 'Who to?' he asked. 'My wife,' I replied. 'She's pregnant, and last time at about this stage she lost the baby.' It was true, but it was intended to appeal to his conscience, and it worked.

It was the Inspector again who took me upstairs to a room with a phone. When Sue answered, I told her I'd been arrested, not to worry, and gave her the address of the police station. I was just about to tell her to contact a solicitor when the officer's hand, hovering over the receiver, clicked the conversation to an end. After I'd left the room he rang back to apologize that the call had been accidentally cut off. It was a mean trick, but at least I had made contact with the outside world.

Far from being swiftly released, we spent two more nights in the uncomfortable cells at Muswell Hill. As we munched bacon sandwiches, smoked cigarettes delivered by friends and read the graffiti on the walls, the news of our arrest hit the headlines. 'Three Held in Secrets Quiz', said one paper; another speculated that we had discussed the Army's pre-detonation of terrorist bombs in Northern Ireland. We hadn't.

In the cramped police station entrance hall, reporters gathered to investigate the mystery. Solicitors arrived to be told they couldn't see us. Messages were refused. Friends met to discuss what could be done, and an Aubrey–Berry–Campbell (conveniently ABC) Defence Committee was quickly formed. Inside, we could hear nothing, except a few shouts of 'Let them out' before some angry friends were hustled away.

Over the weekend we were each led in turn upstairs to an interview room where Chief Superintendent Harry Nicholls of the Special Branch was waiting. As another officer took shorthand notes, Nicholls asked questions about the Friday night interview. Every so often he would play sections from what he clearly considered to be the most 'sensitive' parts of the tape-recording, saying that my voice could be identified by 'voice prints'. At the end, a third officer, seated behind me and hidden from my view, chimed in with the softer 'wouldn't it be easier if you cooperated' line. But my response to all but the most basic inquiries was a variation on 'no comment'. I had asked to see a solicitor and been turned down; I had been kept incommunicado for a day and a half. I was in no mood to be cooperative.

John Berry was given the longest grilling, though the atmosphere was for the most part polite but cool. He rejected Nicholls' suggestion that he had done the interview because he was hard up and needed some money or that he was 'interested in martyrdom'. Duncan Campbell decided to make a statement which merely outlined his journalistic career and specialization.

Almost two days after our arrest, we were finally allowed to see a solicitor. The two lawyers contacted by friends had in fact been phoning the police station alternately every half hour, and were by that stage considering an application for an injunction to force the police to give them access. But at 5 p.m. on Sunday we were taken from the cells, lined up and officially charged under Section 2 of the Official Secrets Act. We were said to have illegally communicated (John Berry) and received (myself and Duncan Campbell) official information. I refused requests for antecedents (background personal history), a photograph and fingerprints. Only my fingerprints were later forced from me – through a court order.

Meanwhile, the Special Branch had been busy with their 'further inquiries'. They had searched my house and John Berry's, whilst a virtual removal service had been sent to Duncan Campbell's Brighton flat. Reference books, novels (including *For Whom The Bell Tolls* and *Brighton Rock*), press cuttings, letters, phone directories, an entire filing-cabinet and even the contents of the waste-paper basket were all bundled into a transit van and taken to the safe-keeping of Scotland Yard. If the police had intended to shatter Duncan's personal and professional life, they could hardly have done it more effectively.

Worse was to come. At Tottenham Magistrates Court on Monday morning we were all refused bail – on the extraordinary argument that we might repeat the alleged offence – and remanded to Brixton Prison. Hisses from the packed public gallery greeted the decision.

Inside Brixton – after the police lost their way again, passing ironically the Old Bailey – we were taken to the maximum security block and locked in separate cells. The association room, to which we were admitted twice a day, had a sinister TV camera in one corner. Our isolation as 'dangerous extremists' also allowed us a special exercise yard, where in ill-fitting brown uniforms we kicked a punctured football beneath a thirty-foot-high fence – and more cameras. We were amused that our prison numbers, B07008, B07009 and B07010, had just missed 007.

Fortunately, it took only a few days for a High Court Judge to be persuaded to overrule Tottenham magistrates. By Wednesday night, Duncan and I were free again, though John Berry stayed inside for a further fortnight. Most people would have found the cost of such an appeal (several hundred pounds in legal fees) prohibitive, but we already had the support of both friends and *Time Out* magazine. Three conditions on our bail said that we must not discuss any details of the interview, report daily to a police station between certain hours and surrender our passports.

Although gruelling enough, that was only the beginning of an even longer ordeal. For several days after my release from prison, I looked in the rear-view mirror of my car for the tell-tale signs of a following vehicle. They were there. But over succeeding months, it was not just the Special Branch who were following the progress of our case. A growing protest began to question the basis of the argument that in one single interview with a retired soldier we had endangered 'the interests of national security'. Before returning to explain how and why our arrest was planned, it is therefore essential to look first at the organizations which defend that concept.

I

In the Interests of National Security

Eighteen months after the arrest of the three of us under the Official Secrets Act, a young Reading student, Guy Smith, received an unexpected visitor at the door of his flat. Flashing a warrant card, the man introduced himself as Detective Constable Mooney and said he would like to ask Smith some questions about his motorbike. 'Where were you on Friday, September 8th at 8 a.m.?' he began. 'You see, a bike like yours was involved in a wages snatch at about that time.' He added that he'd managed to trace Smith's address through the Vehicle Licensing Centre in Swansea.

Smith, whose only recent contact with the police had been to write to them asking for information on their plans for dealing with a major emergency, such as a nuclear attack, was more than a little surprised. He knew nothing about the robbery and had been eating breakfast at the relevant time. His bike, a 125cc Honda, seemed a particularly unlikely getaway vehicle.

But that was not the end of the session. 'How do you pay rent on this flat?' asked the inquisitive detective. 'What sort of work do you do? Research into emergency planning? Why are you interested in that? Who pays for it?' The questioning had moved some way from the wages snatch, but Mooney persisted. After a while he made his excuses and left.

It was only when the policeman had gone that Smith began to ask some serious questions himself. To start with, it seemed odd that the officer had got his present address when the bike was listed at an old London home. Mooney had said that there were twenty suspects for the robbery in Reading alone, yet the Honda carried a Cambridge registration number. Wasn't it also strange that the news had, in Mooney's words, been kept out of the press for 'security reasons'? And what about the timing of the interview – the very day after he'd been told that the police would not be able to help him with his research inquiries.

Guy Smith didn't have to wait long for an explanation. When he phoned Reading police station to take up the point about his address he was told that Mooney was not in the ordinary CID. He was a member of the Special Branch.

Over the next few days Mooney fumbled his way through two different explanations as to how he had located Smith's flat. Though plausible, neither rang particularly true. When Smith complained about his treatment he eventually received a written apology for the whole incident from an Assistant Chief Constable in the Thames Valley Police. He had been interviewed 'under the pretext of an entirely fictitious matter', the letter explained. The robbery had never happened. But though the police apologized for the method of their approach, they still considered their probing of the 'authenticity and intentions' of people like Guy Smith to be justified.

In fact, Smith's experience was unusual only because of the ineptitude of the approach. The basic operation of intelligence-gathering is common practice. The Special Branch's files, now being transferred on to a new computer in South London, record the names of over 1.25 million individuals. Six years ago, these were expanding at the rate of 2,000 new names every month.[1] Many of those included are there not because they have committed any offence, but because at some stage, like Smith, they were considered 'undesirable'.

Who the Special Branch considers undesirable has ranged in the past from Irish militants to suffragettes, from nuclear disarmers to a campaign for the rights of illegitimate children, from school teachers to Welsh Nationalists. However minor their action at the time, they are all seen as potential trouble-makers. 'The function of the Special Branch in official language is to guard the security of the State', as the *Daily Express* reported over forty years ago. 'But the men themselves have another name for it. They say their job is to clear up political nuisances.'

The Branch's ability to do that has increased enormously over the last two decades. In the early 1960s there were just 200 Special Branch officers based in London. Now there are at

1. *New Scientist*, 18.1.79.

least 1,250,[1] a third of those in the capital. Every provincial police authority has developed its own Special Branch team, ranging in strength from a handful to sixty officers, and all in regular contact with the centre of information-gathering and collation – New Scotland Yard.

Official justification for this growth in manpower has usually centred on the threat of Irish terrorism. When it was formed in the 1880s the unit was originally called the Special Irish Branch. But although the Republican movement is still extremely active, the police have adapted to meet its challenge. There is now not only a 70-strong Irish section within the London Special Branch but also a separate Anti-Terrorist Squad. In Northern Ireland, the Royal Ulster Constabulary has its own Special Branch of 279 men and women.[2] For a Home Secretary pressed to explain a sixfold increase in Britain's political police, terrorism is guaranteed to win emotional support, but it by no means accounts for the majority of the Special Branch's activities.

From its headquarters on the top floor of New Scotland Yard, the Branch has responsibility for guarding visiting dignitaries and Cabinet Ministers, keeping a 24-hour watch on all ports and airports, vetting every application for naturalization as a British citizen (it sometimes uses the cover name 'Nationality Department'), maintaining records on overseas visitors and immigrants, providing security for foreign embassies, as well as the pervasive work of surveilling 'subversive' organizations. It also makes the arrests and investigates any offences under the Official Secrets Act.

During the course of a year, a Branch officer may find himself standing at the shoulder of an immigration officer at Dover, listening to the interminable progress of a political meeting or poring over photographs taken at a demonstration. It is often tedious and boring work, but it's all material for the files – white for an initial reference, green for a file opened, red for active surveillance.

The current boss is 50-year-old Colin Hewett, one of whose predecessors was said to have a black box on the wall for making

1. Figure given by the Home Secretary in the House of Commons, 24.5.78.
2. Figure given by the Northern Ireland Secretary in the House of Commons, 13.6.78.

'scrambled' (not easily decipherable) phone calls to the Home Office. Around him in the open-plan offices are filing-cabinets full of dossiers on groups and individuals: even favourite pubs and holiday spots are listed. On the notice-boards are leaflets distributed by organizations being watched, photos of incidents and cartoons attacking the secret police. At Hewett's disposal is a virtual Hertz service of vans, taxis and cars; only a handful of ordinary police vehicles are used.

Though recruits come direct from the regular police, the Special Branch men are not typical coppers. Before joining, they are thoroughly checked out through references and personal histories, and are expected to be bright enough to adopt the dress and manners of whatever circle they are moving in. Unlike the CID, they are trained to look for political background and ideas rather than direct 'evidence' of a crime. Although their qualifications are supposed to include good shorthand and at least one foreign language, their greatest skill is to observe and remain unnoticed.

Much Branch information in fact originates from comparatively open sources. Petitions sent to government departments are examined for likely names, newspapers read[1] and photos cut out, leaflets collected and subscriptions opened through a box number on a wide range of publications. When a particularly interesting issue of a magazine is published, a Branch man will buy up the statutory half-dozen copies from a left-wing bookshop such as Collets in Charing Cross Road. His extravagance inevitably marks him out.

At large public meetings, especially on political and industrial issues, a Special Branch officer will be in the crowd – watching who attends and who speaks, and taking shorthand notes of what is said. At smaller gatherings the local police do the footwork. According to official instructions they then pass on their notes of 'inflammatory' speeches or 'those of special interest' or 'disorder of any kind' to the Branch.[2]

1. The Special Branch is said to note every name in a number of left-wing newspapers, especially the Communist *Morning Star*.

2. General Orders for the Metropolitan Police, quoted in *Time Out*, 20.9.74.

Collecting information on political events in London has now become so routine that a special form, like an accident report, has been devised by Scotland Yard, and organizers are asked for the names and addresses of speakers, subject matter and dates of further meetings. One London police division, Greenwich, has admitted that it tries to check on *every* political meeting in its area for 'public order' purposes.[1] Projected nationally, with hundreds of events each week on everything from union disputes to abortion, this is a mammoth task. And in law there is no requirement for anybody to cooperate with such requests.

At the same time, regular approaches are made to employers, doctors or government officials for snippets of information. Local journalists, with their detailed knowledge of groups and personalities, provide a useful source of intelligence. The Special Branch man will drop in for a chat, as though on a social visit, and only occasionally ask for the address of someone who's written a letter to the paper or the names of people who attended a trade union meeting. A crime reporter may even be asked to find out information himself in exchange for preferential treatment from his police contacts, perhaps passing on unpublished photos from a demonstration.

One provincial journalist recalled the unannounced arrival of a Special Branch man in his office one quiet lunchtime. 'He said he was keeping a watch on subversive individuals and organizations and wanted to know about shop stewards, the Campaign for Nuclear Disarmament and even tenants' associations. He asked us to keep an eye on these people and let him know of anything we could find out – what they were saying, what they were doing. I think he assumed that we were solid, establishment characters because we were working for a *Daily Telegraph*-type newspaper. He didn't realize that the two of us in the office were in fact socialists.'

Even the publicly admitted duties of the Special Branch can be used to gather an extensive range of information. Three hundred officers, some brought in from the CID, are permanently attached to sea and airports, picked for their ability never

1. *Time Out*, 18.5.79.

to forget a face. With the aid of a thick black book containing brief personal descriptions they can oversee the travels of thousands of individuals, whether gun-runners or political activists. For example, one American, Louis Wolf, who visits Britain regularly, was held overnight in Heathrow Airport's detention centre simply because of his entry in this book – and then allowed to enter the country for a limited period only.[1] The entry recorded no more than his 'association' with Philip Agee, whose hounding by the security agencies will be described later. Through immigration officers, with whom they cooperate closely, the Special Branch also claims the legal right to read and copy any papers or documents brought into the country. This power is regularly used.

On other occasions more insidious methods will be used. Protest marches are photographed for the 'album' and regular meeting places of organizations watched. For instance, during the long-running Grunwick factory dispute in North London, the offices of the local Trades Council were surveyed from hired rooms in a nearby pub.[2]

Whenever a particular crime is under investigation, the Special Branch will raid the homes and offices of large numbers of people with only the vaguest association with those considered responsible.[3] Though in some cases they will be looking for specific evidence, in others these are merely 'fishing expeditions'. The sprats they catch are address books, diaries, notes and letters, all carted away for transcribing and (possible) return. A series of visits of this type followed the arrest of the three of us (see Chapter 2).

And behind this relatively open process is the network of informers, whether innocently or deliberately passing on what they know. Their motive may be bitterness or a genuine sense of duty or quite simply that the police know something about them that they would rather not have exposed. But it is from the

1. Reported in the *Guardian*, 28.12.79; *Time Out*, 11.1.80.

2. *New Statesman*, 1.2.80.

3. See a description of the raids during the 1978–9 'anarchists' case in *Persons Unknown*, booklet available from Box 123, 182 Upper Street, London N1.

ranks of the informers that the *agents provocateurs* are most likely to emerge.

It was the suggestion by a Special Branch informer that an Irish welfare organization should start collecting weapons which led to the arrest of five people in 1971 on charges of conspiracy to possess firearms. However, when the role of the 'helpful Irishman' was described in court, the case was suddenly dropped. It later emerged that some of the guns supplied to the Irish group had previously been in police custody, whilst the 'Irishman' himself had been an informer for twenty years. But attempts at the trial to elicit more information about him met with the rebuff that 'it would prejudice the security of the state'. The same blank wall met inquiries about phone-tapping and secret photography of the accused.[1]

Kenneth Lennon, the most dramatic example of an *agent provocateur*, was, to start with at least, more successful. As a Branch informer on Irish Republicans in Luton, he helped set up the conviction of three men for conspiracy to rob. He had been promised payment on 'results achieved', and his reward was a lump sum of £100 (in 1973) and then £20 a month from the Branch's Information Fund.

The following year he in turn encouraged another man to try to 'break' one of the three from Winson Green prison in Birmingham. Both were arrested during a reconnoitre of the gaol, but while his accomplice got three years, the evidence against Lennon was blatantly insufficient. Not only was he described as 'honest and frank' and his record said to be clean (untrue), but his role in the attempted break-in was deliberately underplayed.

This crude attempt by the Special Branch to protect its own proved Lennon's eventual downfall. Three weeks after his acquittal, he made a conscience-stricken statement to the National Council for Civil Liberties in which he said he had been originally recruited because of his sister Bernadette's sympathies with the Provisional IRA. As far as he was concerned it was blackmail. Two days later he was found shot dead

1. See the *Sunday Times*, 18.6.72, and the book *Reluctant Judas* by Geoff Robertson (Temple Smith, 1976).

in a quiet Surrey lane. Nobody was ever caught for the murder, and the official inquiry into the Lennon affair completely exonerated the Branch's role.[1]

The position of *agents provocateurs* has in fact never been adequately clarified. The police use them when they think appropriate, and the courts accept their evidence. There is no legal defence of 'entrapment', as in the United States. As one judge commented on the original 'Luton Three' case with which Kenneth Lennon was involved: 'It is no defence for an accused to prove that he would not have committed the offence without the urging or assistance of a police spy.'

At a more mundane level, an informer was discovered to have moved in with a group of people producing political leaflets and newspapers from a 'squat' in Bristol. The man was at first friendly, energetic and positively militant when it came to discussing a proposed demonstration. But when some people from the house were arrested after a raid, they found their friend waiting for them at the police station. He said 'he had just decided to join the police force' and left hurriedly.[2] 'By a system of informers and undercover men, the Branch knows all that is going on in the fringe organizations of the left and right', as the *Daily Telegraph* noted in 1964.

Who the Special Branch considers worthy of surveillance depends on its judgement of the political situation at the time. Twenty years ago it was the Campaign for Nuclear Disarmament (and the more militant Committee of 100), a movement which pioneered the peaceful sit-down and opposed by marches and publicity the creation of a British nuclear capacity. Large numbers of people shared their horror at the potential for human destruction contained in one small bomb, and their successors can now be found returning to the theme as well as exposing the dangers of 'peaceful' nuclear energy.

But to the Branch this was a protest of an unprecedented type which embraced both middle- and working-class supporters. During the growth of CND activities, observation of the cam-

1. A full account of the Lennon affair is given in *Reluctant Judas* (see preceding footnote).
2. *New Statesman*, 26.4.74.

paign even included collecting the names and addresses of those involved in small church hall gatherings.[1] At the same time phones were tapped, letters opened and homes raided.[2] A village shopkeeper found herself cornered behind the counter one day and asked about her 18-year-old son, then secretary of the local CND group. 'He might be a security risk', she was told, though he had committed no identifiable offence.[3]

Of crucial importance to our own prosecution was the arrest of six people in 1961 just before a planned sit-down at a nuclear air base in Wethersfield, Suffolk. They were all charged and tried under Section 1 of the Official Secrets Act – the first time the supposed 'spying' clause had been used otherwise.[4] Many years later, the ABC case was the second. But for the nuclear protest movement, the eventual conviction of the six was clearly a political move to disarm and demoralize.

In the late 1960s it was the turn of the black community to be placed under observation.[5] Though black people had quite rightly been concerned about discrimination and the effect of Enoch Powell's inflammatory speeches, to the Branch their emerging organizations were lumped together as some form of Black Power. Few meetings of black groups during this period would start without reference to the believed police spy among their number. The Branch's job was partly to encourage divisive splits and personality clashes, partly to chart activities and partly to make everyone so nervous that they were always looking over their shoulder.

At the same time, considerable attention was being paid to a completely different group, the Welsh Nationalists. Interest in a party which has since had MPs elected to parliament reached its height at the time of Prince Charles's investiture as Prince of Wales in 1969. Local police forces were asked for full details

1. *Reynolds News*, 30.6.57.
2. One Committee of 100 group produced a pamphlet, *Mail Interception and Telephone Tapping in Britain*, recording some of its experiences.
3. *Civil Liberty*, 10.62.
4. For a description of the case see *Not In the Public Interest* by David Williams (Hutchinson, 1965). Section 1 charges were also brought in the *Isis* case (see page 140), but were dropped during a plea bargain.
5. See *Police Power and Black People* by Derek Humphry (Panther, 1972).

(name, address, date of birth, car number) of anybody even sympathetic to Welsh nationalism. Plaid Cymru alone had 40,000 members then, but the tailing by car, the snaps for the album and the listing of names continued over a lengthy period.

These are only examples of areas that have been targeted by the Special Branch at different times. A permanent undercurrent of its work is interest in any organization to the left, and occasionally to the right, of the political spectrum. But in recent years the Branch has spread its net so widely that it is difficult to crudely categorize. Though publicity is something it shuns, the number of cases where surveillance has been revealed, as opposed to remaining hidden, has now reached disturbing proportions.

Within industry, Special Branch officers have been discovered supplying information to factory managements on workers involved in disputes, a clear indication of their interest in legal trade union activity. As Tony Bunyan explains in his book, *The Political Police in Britain*, 'what is to the trade unionist legitimate activity in furtherance of a pay claim or against an arbitrary management decision becomes, in the eyes of the Branch, industrial unrest led by politically motivated militants.' During a strike in 1973 at a Hampshire factory making Ford van bodies, for example, the company's chief accountant admitted making several visits to the Branch's office in Southampton to exchange information. One officer was even allowed to tour the factory posing as a commercial traveller. Several people were identified by the Branch as 'ringleaders' of the strike, though no criminal offence was alleged.[1] The *Daily Telegraph* quoted Special Branch sources as saying such investigations were 'not unusual. They constitute an important part of detectives' work.'

Four years later, during an occupation against closure of a British Steel subsidiary in Greenwich, the workers came across Special Branch reports on two of their colleagues. One referred to a minor offence twenty years before. The other listed several complaints for 'political activities' against shop steward Paul Lutener, including 'taking part in illegal demonstrations'. As yet, demonstrations are not against the law. 'We are advised by experts to keep meticulous records of anything that happens

1. *Sunday Times*, 14.4.74.

concerning certain individuals so we can build up a dossier', the management noted in a confidential memorandum. Lutener himself was eventually sacked – for taking part in a demonstration.[1]

Students have been regularly approached to supply information on their friends and associates, as in 1977 when Robert MacNeill, a first-year student at Paisley College of Technology, was asked to see the college secretary after a lecture. Ushered into another room where a middle-aged man was waiting, he was shown a police identity card and asked if he could help with 'secret and confidential information'. For his services as a spy on other students, MacNeill was promised tax-free payments – and a copy of the Official Secrets Act to sign. He refused both.[2] 'It reminded me of 1984,' he said afterwards. 'I was disgusted and frightened. I never imagined this could happen.'

MacNeill was singled out because his father was a civilian driver with Edinburgh City Police. He was therefore considered reliable. But another student, Tony McRoy, who was in his second year at Hull University studying politics, experienced more subtle pressure. McRoy was arrested in Hull in February 1979 under the Prevention of Terrorism Act (he was an admitted member of the Political Section of the Ulster Defence Association). During heavy questioning about his alleged connection to terrorist activities, however, it was pointed out that he was also a member of the National Front. 'If we tell the students, life for you will be hard,' he was warned. 'You will probably have to leave university.' McRoy's expected response was to become a police informer, and over the next few days he was asked to identify marked faces in photos of demonstrations, to infiltrate the students union and to phone a special number whenever any political action was planned at the university. With the threat of revelation of his National Front membership hanging over him, McRoy says he 'had no bloody choice', though he was not charged with any offence.[3]

1. *Socialist Worker*, 21.5.77.
2. *Guardian*, 9.2.78.
3. Details from a statement by McRoy to a Greater Manchester Police inquiry.

Other recent examples of Special Branch activity include their checking of the enrolment list at a further education class on 'Great Marxist Writers',[1] a tour of Sussex schools asking about the political leanings of teachers[2] and extensive surveillance at the 1977 annual conference of a left-wing political party. Delegates were photographed as they arrived at the railway station and then local hotels were asked to note down the names and addresses of all those attending.[3] Though official inquiries have been instituted in some of these cases, there is little evidence that the Branch's practice has changed.

What use is made of all this mass of information? In terms of employment, it can result in a job not offered, a promotion deferred or even the sack. One teacher, David Ruddell, found his career dogged after a mysterious phone conversation between the Special Branch and a prospective employer during which an officer referred to 'Hammer and Sickle business'. Hammer and Sickle – the Communist symbol – is police shorthand for politically undesirable, though Ruddell could think of nothing in his past (he was a member of the Labour Party) to warrant such a label.[4] In 1975, a South London garage attendant was sacked after a local police officer told the manager that the Branch suspected him of being an IRA fund-raiser.) Not only was there no truth in the allegation, but by the time his union representative had checked out the source Morris had lost his opportunity to appeal to an industrial tribunal.

For political groups it can mean the singling out of individuals at a demonstration or meeting for arrest on minor charges such as obstruction. The exhausting and diverting effect such cases can have on a protest is not lost on the Branch. When the editor of the *Yorkshire Miner* newspaper, Maurice Jones, was arrested on a trade union picket line in 1977, he had his personal life history repeated to him from a file and was given the sinister warning: 'You have a delightful little girl, Mr Jones. The roads

1. *Guardian*, 7.10.77.
2. *Sussex Express*, 18.3.77.
3. *Guardian*, 6.4.77.
4. *New Statesman*, 7.10.73.
5. *Socialist Worker*, 29.3.75.

become very busy at this time of the year.' Jones fled the country in panic.[1]

And it is the subtle injection of details about a person's political views which can turn the minds of a judge and jury in an apparently non-political trial. The Special Branch do not often appear in court, but their files do. According to the General Orders for the Metropolitan Police, 'whenever persons are arrested for offences connected with political activities, including minor breaches of the peace and cases of slogan-daubing etc., inquiry is always to be made to the Special Branch to ascertain whether anything is known about the accused *before* the case is dealt with at Court.' What is known is likely to be political views or activities, officially nothing to do with a charge of, say, obstruction.

To many people it may seem bad enough that a record of their personal views and lifestyle is on file at all – especially if it is inaccurate. After all, no political organization is currently illegal in this country. As Labour MP Neil Kinnock protested during the course of the ABC case: 'The police must be denied the licence to use their professional position for the pursuit of private, political, religious or moral beliefs.' In practice, that is exactly the sort of information the Special Branch collects.

If the work of the Special Branch sounds extensive and all-seeing, this is only because it is the most public arm of the security machine. Its officers have names and occasionally faces. But behind it is another organization – far larger, far more secretive and far less likely to expose its mistakes. When the teacher discovered the sinister reference to 'Hammer and Sickle business', the original warning did not come from the police. It came from Box 500. To the initiated, Box 500 is the cryptic security code for MI5.

Also known as the Security Service, MI5 employs an estimated 4–5,000 people from at least six central London offices, mostly in Mayfair.[2] These include a floor of the prominent Euston Tower block, noticeable for its permanently drawn

1. *Morning Star*, 18.7.77.
2. Listed in the *New Statesman*, 8.2.80.

curtains. Its headquarters building in Curzon Street is distinguished only by a jutting concrete parapet designed to deflect an explosion in the street below. Though one building worker claimed to have discovered, during refurbishment work in 1975, an underground area divided into dozens of small cubicles,[1] no sign-board indicates what goes on behind the iron-grilled windows. A similar anonymity surrounds much of MI5's daily operations.

With its military-sounding name, it is commonly assumed that this secrecy has to do with catching spies. MI5 owes it origin to a German spy scare before the First World War, and its activities have mostly come to light since then over major cases of espionage. But this is only part of its job. It also advises on security within government departments, is called in on any alleged violation of the Official Secrets Act and actively investigates potential 'subversives', whether in the civil service or outside. Just as much as the Special Branch it is a watchdog over political and personal views.

But while the Branch is more concerned with short-term surveillance, MI5 takes a longer view. Its agents will work under cover in a factory for many years, listening to what people say and even joining a political party. It has permanent contacts on the staff of many academic institutions, as well as among students. When MI5 taps a phone, it is for months rather than weeks.

The relationship between the two organizations is nonetheless close. Branch officers are often called the 'running boys' for MI5: they make the crucial phone call, do the interviews, carry out the arrests, whilst the Security Service provides the background, passing on only the most essential information. (MI5 in fact has no powers of arrest itself.) Its filing system, known as the Central Registry, is reported to contain several million names,[2] and even a sympathetic observer has described it as a 'large and complex organization which can touch the life of every citizen'.[3]

Those who work, or apply to work, in government depart-

1. *Workers Press*, 2.7.75.

2. For example, by Chapman Pincher in *Inside Story* (Sidgwick and Jackson, 1978).

3. John Bulloch in *MI5* (Barker, 1963).

ments, especially those concerned with defence, are the most likely to come under MI5's microscope. All major Ministries have their own security sections, but MI5 is the central authority to which inquiries are made. Its files provide the vital evidence about a person's 'suspect' views and its officers assist in the more sophisticated process of 'positive vetting' – building up a total picture of an employee's personal and political life.

How this vetting works and how it is partly used to discourage the disclosure of embarrassing information will be explained later (see Chapter 4). But in general, anyone with the remotest connection to a left-wing organization is liable to be weeded out and not appointed, quietly sacked or moved to another job. In the 1950s, at the height of the McCarthy witch-hunt in America, many thousands of people were investigated by MI5 and the military security departments. Anger at the abuse of this system even led then to the emergence of a Campaign for the Limitation of Secret Police Powers.

Of equal concern is the surveillance of individuals outside government. MI5 collects, for example, regular reports on trade union activities,[1] some of which are forwarded secretly to Cabinet Ministers – in theory to help them judge the political climate of industrial relations. Former Employment Minister Barbara Castle recorded in her memoirs how the Security Service supplied frequent briefings, including one on a purported relationship between engineering union leader Hugh Scanlon and the Communist Party.

At the same time, immigration officers are given detailed instructions to inform Box 500 of anybody who has travelled to or studied in a Communist country or is found carrying 'subversive literature'. MI5 has its own section of the black book mentioned earlier, also known as the Suspects Index, where 1,000 selected individuals are given special 'action codes'. Immigration officers are told to question these people closely and then telephone the Box 500 duty officer. They can also use

---

1. Extracts from a report on a shop steward at Carnation Foods in Dumfries were published in *Time Out*, 25.7.80. Prepared for MI5 by the local Special Branch, it showed careful monitoring of the man's union involvement.

MI5's telex machine, which answers back with the code 'Snuff-box'.[1]

As with the Special Branch, students, seen as the potential leaders and rebels of the future, provide a regular hunting-ground. They are viewed both as possible recruits and as informers on their colleagues' activities. After one Cambridge student had followed up a comparatively open recruitment letter with an expenses-paid trip to Whitehall, he was told at an interview what was needed: 'A report from time to time on the political actions and attitudes of some undergraduates, and occasionally a full report in reply to a specific inquiry'. More often, such approaches are made discreetly through a friend, and a thorough security check done first.

Not all attempts at intelligence-gathering are so direct. A former MI5 employee has described the tools of his trade as miniature tape-recorders, bugging devices and telephoto-lens cameras. On special jobs they used vans with blacked-out windows for close-quarters surveillance; inside, there were receivers to record conversations from a bugged meeting room. The technique of letter-opening was actually pioneered by the Security Service during the First World War.

Such methods are said to be used regularly to monitor trade union activities. During the 1971 miners' strike an agent managed to plant a briefcase fitted with a tape-recorder in a cafe where leading members of the National Union of Miners were talking. Many trade union headquarters are believed to have bugs concealed in their walls, ready for activation during an industrial dispute. One such device was discovered built into a wall when the Communist Party's head office in Covent Garden was re-decorated during 1975.[2]

Even MPs are not immune from MI5 surveillance. Every new member is placed on file in the Registry, using the argument that they may at some time be subject to espionage approaches. In the early 1960s the Labour Party leadership, spearheaded by Hugh Gaitskell, George Brown and Patrick Gordon Walker, even

1. *Guardian*, 24.10.79; *New Statesman*, 2.11.79.
2. *The Times*, 8.2.75. Technological methods of surveillance are described in more detail in Chapter 2.

gave the Security Service a free hand to tap the telephones, open the mail and examine the bank accounts of fifteen MPs it suspected of 'fellow-travelling' with the Communists.[1] The results have never been revealed. But when an inquisitive Member asked the Home Secretary more recently whether he could look at his Box 500 file, he was told: 'You would find it not worth reading.'[2] Why then, he might have replied, is it there?

Only occasionally do the results of these investigations emerge. It was on the basis of reports from what he called 'operators in the field' that Prime Minister Harold Wilson made his notorious remark during the 1966 seamen's strike to the effect that it was being manipulated by 'a tightly-knit group of politically motivated men'. He later explained this had meant Communists, though not one member of the union's national executive was in fact a member of the party. In practice, MI5's intelligence, allegedly from bugging and intercepted documents, was used by the Labour government to defuse a particularly disruptive strike.[3]

This potentially fragile relationship between governments and the Security Service, to which I shall return at the end of this chapter, was further emphasized during the last years of Harold Wilson's premiership. A series of incidents – including confusion in MI5 files between two Cabinet Ministers, Judith Hart and David Owen, and two other people with similar names – suggested that all was not well between the country's leaders and the secret bureaucracy. The most dramatic of these was the allegation that Wilson himself had actually been bugged by MI5 both in Downing Street and in his private room at the House of Commons.[4] The suggested reason was the ubiquitous possibility of 'Communist infiltration', and the technicians were said to come from Government Communications Headquarters (GCHQ) in Cheltenham. Interestingly, the work of GCHQ was

1. See *Inside Story* by Chapman Pincher.
2. Alex Lyon in the House of Commons, 5.4.78.
3. See *The Labour Government 1964–1970* by Harold Wilson (Penguin, 1974) and *Inside Story* by Chapman Pincher.
4. *Daily Express*, 29.7.77 and 30.7.77.

the subject of the conversation between myself, Duncan Campbell and John Berry.

That the Security Service had even considered surveillance of its supposed political master was sensational enough. But the speculation thrown out by the incident raised an important question mark over MI5's political neutrality. At one stage, responsibility for the bugging was placed on a 'right-wing faction' within the organization.

Whatever the truth of that theory, MI5 still retains the atmosphere of an establishment club, a remnant of its colonial past. At one time its work covered all Commonwealth countries, as well as Britain. Even now, its recruits come largely from the civil service, army and police (though also from professionals such as economists and psychologists), are expected to be British-born and must accept a paternalistic structure in which loyalty is more important than financial reward. Its present head is Sir Howard Smith, previously British Ambassador in Moscow. Those who leave have been able to return to powerful jobs in private industry and the public service; one ex-MI5 man is now a High Court judge, another head of a multinational computer firm's public relations department.

By contrast with the Special Branch, the operations of the Security Service are literally above the law. MI5's existence is not recognized by any legislation, not even the Official Secrets Act.[1] How much money it costs to run and even the name of its Director-General are kept secret, and the ignorance of the general public is both supported and then meekly criticized by successive political leaders, fearful of themselves being labelled disloyal.

Alongside MI5 at the top of the secret hierarchy there is also the most anonymous of the British spying organizations – MI6. Officially, it doesn't even exist. According to public records its operations came to an abrupt conclusion at the end of the Second World War – over thirty years ago. In practice it is still very much in business, and just as MI5 has retreated from the shrinking Empire, so MI6 (also called the Secret Service) has expanded.

1. Explained in Lord Denning's Report on the Profumo scandal, 1963.

With the task of collecting intelligence and organizing spying *outside* Britain, it technically spans the world.

At every major British embassy abroad one or two diplomats will in fact be working for MI6. Their intelligence – on politics, economics and important personalities – is gathered both direct and through paid agents, invariably nationals of the country concerned. These include businessmen, civil servants and military officials, all dealt with through 'cut-outs' or intermediaries. The system is similar to that of the Central Intelligence Agency (CIA), the very much larger American counterpart to which MI6 originally offered its expertise,[1] and in both organizations these embassy units are known as 'stations'.

Like the CIA, MI6 doesn't only operate in countries openly hostile to Britain. It is as much concerned to know what a close ally is planning, or whether a developing country in the Third World will achieve an economic stability sympathetic to British investment. Anti-communism is inevitably part of its credo. In theory at least, any potentially embarrassing clandestine operations in furtherance of those ends, such as bugging or burglaries, are supposed to be approved by the local ambassador.

The administrative centre of MI6 is Century House, a twenty-storey office block just south of the Thames in London.[2] Six hundred people work there, and it is officially described as the Research Department of the Foreign Office. Its Director-General is still known as 'C', a tradition dating from the very first holder of the office, Captain Mansfield Cummings. The present incumbent, 61-year-old Sir Arthur Franks, has responsibility for MI6's five Directorates, each dealing with a different aspect of collecting and analysing intelligence, and for its vast filing system, said to include both foreign spies and some alleged 'subversives' inside Britain. The Secret Service also has training centres in London and Hampshire, and a separate London 'station' in Vauxhall Bridge Road.

MI6 stations abroad keep in touch with Century House using their own special codes and cyphers. Official letters to the agency are sent to the mythical figure of G. H. Merrick, a long-standing

1. See Chapter 3 for a description of the CIA's operations.
2. For a peep inside Century House see *Time Out*, 22.7.77.

code-name. But eventually a selected digest of its intelligence will be passed on to the Foreign Office, to which MI6 is technically responsible. Though often containing little more than political gossip, these digests are still classified, stamped in red and transported in locked boxes.

In one respect at least, MI6 does intrude on to British territory. In London, it cooperates with MI5 (through a liaison office in Gower Street, W1) on the task of scrutinizing all visiting diplomats at 'suspect' foreign embassies. Personal details, especially drinking habits and sexual orientation, are carefully noted and filed away in counter-intelligence files. In Secret Service jargon, these files are known as Box 850. Concern about contact between British citizens and Communist countries even extends to checking the flight lists of Soviet bloc airlines. How many holiday-makers have found their way into Box 850 isn't known.

MI6 also has important links with two other organizations within the secret world, both of which are important to an understanding of the ABC case. One is Government Communications Headquarters in Cheltenham, on which the Secret Service depends for the results of world-wide electronic eavesdropping. This massive network will be described in more detail in Chapter 5, but there is little doubt that John Berry's description of its work would have equally angered the Century House bureaucracy.

The other is the American CIA. Just as MI6 officers are known as 'The Friends', so the CIA are nicknamed 'The Cousins'. The relationship is close, with the clear political aim of maintaining Western dominance in its chosen spheres of influence. It also ensures that the two agencies don't tread on each other's toes.

Day-to-day contact with the Americans is made through the United States Embassy in London, which conceals a large CIA station of some fifty officers, and via the MI6 equivalent in Washington. A CIA officer visits Century House every day, and it is through such channels that the information to discredit Philip Agee, eventually leading to his deportation, would have been passed on to the British authorities. As I have explained, it was Agee's arbitrary treatment, along with fellow American Mark Hosenball, which resulted indirectly in our own arrest.

Given the official denial even of its existence, it is hardly surprising that little has emerged about the postwar activities of MI6. It has never been subjected to the same rigorous scrutiny as the CIA, though its responsibilities are parallel. Those who defend its position in the security hierarchy say this is quite simply because it has never been involved in the same level of 'dirty tricks'. Investigators are more sceptical. Bernard Nossiter, former London correspondent of the *Washington Post*, claims that British Intelligence 'stage-manages coups, burgles safes, blackmails the vulnerable and practises most of the other curious arts familiar to well-endowed agencies with overseas interests'.

What amounts to a dirty trick is obviously a matter of opinion. But MI6 has certainly been involved in a number of operations the result of which has been the overthrow of what were considered to be politically unacceptable regimes: these include the government of Dr Mossadegh in Iran (1953), heralding the lengthy tenancy of the Shah,[1] and the People's Progressive Party in the former British colony of Guyana, which fell in 1964 after a manipulated general strike.[2] In both cases, there was close cooperation with the CIA, which actually funded the Guyanan strike.

More recently, MI6 is said to have supported the CIA's intervention in the 1976 Angolan civil war, arranging the supply of long-distance radios to the eventually defeated right-wing UNITA faction, as well as medical treatment for wounded soldiers in London clinics. Not only was a blind eye turned to British mercenaries who chose to fight there, but intelligence officers even accompanied them on trips.[3] The official government position during the Angolan crisis was one of neutrality.

The extent of MI6's international network was also shown by

1. *Observer*, 12.8.79. A detailed account of the planning of this joint CIA/MI6 coup has recently been given by the ex-CIA field commander in Tehran. See the *Guardian*, 28.7.80.

2. *Sunday Times*, 16.4.67 and 23.4.67

3. *Scotsman*, 5.8.78; *People's News Service*, 1.8.78 and 5.9.78.

the investigations of two Swedish journalists in the early 1970s. They discovered cooperation between Swedish and British intelligence on such things as a fortnightly briefing service, the surveillance of individuals and a jointly planned break-in at the South African legation in Stockholm.

Such revelations have only come to light through leaks, journalistic investigations or the much more open attitude to secrecy in the United States. Last year, for instance, an American TV reporter discovered that British intelligence agents had used letter-opening, bugging, safe-cracking, forged documents and kidnaps to defuse the movement against United States involvement in the Second World War.[1] Over forty years later, that information is still secret in this country. In fact just once in recent times has any official British government recognition been given to the work of MI6 and then, during what was known as the Littlejohn affair, reluctantly.

The two Littlejohn brothers – Kenneth and Keith – hit the headlines in 1973 when they were sentenced to a total of thirty-five years' gaol for a £67,000 bank robbery in Dublin. At their trial they made the astonishing claim that they were set up for the job by British intelligence – as part of a campaign to discredit the IRA.

Although both had criminal records, Kenneth Littlejohn was put in touch with 'the appropriate authorities' after a meeting between his brother and an aristocratic prison visitor, Lady Onslow, and a subsequent approach to himself by the then Parliamentary Under-Secretary at the Ministry of Defence, Geoffrey Johnson-Smith. The brothers said they were subsequently given immunity from prosecution (Kenneth Littlejohn was wanted for an English bank raid) and set to work to infiltrate the Republican movement.

During their brief year as agents, they claimed to have bombed two police stations, been handed a gun by their MI6 contact and been shown a hit-list of IRA leaders. But when they were arrested for the Dublin bank robbery their hopes of seeking sanctuary with their paymasters proved vain. Their criminal antics had apparently gone too far, and they were disowned.

1. *Guardian*, 21.8.79.

Despite attempts by the British government to hush up the affair, partly by holding extradition hearings for the brothers (from Britain to Eire) in secret on the grounds of 'national security', a parliamentary row broke out. Home Secretary Robert Carr eventually admitted that Kenneth Littlejohn *had* been working with MI6 and was in touch with a Chief Inspector Sinclair of the Special Branch.[1] Any approval for illegal activities or immunity from court proceedings was still denied by the government, and demands for a formal inquiry were rejected because of 'a long-established rule that we do not discuss the activities of the intelligence services in public'.

This expected closing of the doors left numerous questions unanswered. Was it common practice for people with both criminal records and charges pending to be recruited by the Secret Service? What instructions had the Littlejohns really been given? And was it true, as the brothers alleged, that part of MI6's work had been to precipitate through bomb outrages the introduction of stronger anti-terrorist laws in the Republic? As an Irish politician commented at the time: 'The whole affair stinks.'

Even at Century House, the odour of suspicion surrounding the Littlejohn affair was not lost. A directive went round stating baldly that MI6 does not indulge in violence, and certainly not assassinations. (In fact, 'termination with extreme prejudice', the MI6 jargon for assassinations, is said to have been attempted several times in the past against foreign political figures.) The directive was intended to bolster morale, but also no doubt to reinforce the constant concern that nothing must ever leak out.

Precautions against such leaks are extensive. All staff at Century House are security-vetted, work in separate self-contained areas and are taught even to dispose of typewriter carbons in special waste bags. Guards patrol with walkie-talkie radios, and officers making searches in sensitive files are literally locked in until they call to be let out. Getting rid of waste paper is taken so seriously that a special disposal room has an electronic

1. In a letter to Lord Wigg, 13.8.73.

beam inside and a panel of lights to indicate a breach of security. When the system breaks down, the paper has to be burned instead.

It is a strange, enclosed world, very far from the swashbuckling image of James Bond. Cocktails on palm-fringed beaches have little place in the MI6 officer's routine. But if the role of MI6 is in fact more hard-nosed – the protection of Western international interests by clandestine methods – it is not above using that position to disarm those it considers to be a nuisance. Among the nuisances will be anybody who tries to investigate further than the bland public statements that the national security is being protected.

Those, then, are three powerful agencies of 'national security' which, in one way or another, influenced the progress of the ABC case. A fourth, GCHQ, will make an appearance later in this account. It is also worth mentioning that the three armed forces – Navy, Army and Air Force – have their own intelligence arms, both defensive (concerned with internal security) and aggressive. Their efforts are coordinated by the Defence Intelligence Staff (DIS) department at the Ministry of Defence, and the importance of DIS to the ABC case was emphasized by the fact that the anonymous Colonel B, a key figure in our prosecution (see Chapter 5), had worked there.

But if the impression has been given that a considerable amount is known about what these organizations do, then this is unfortunately false. It is invariably only through their mistakes, or the persistent inquiries of investigators, that anything emerges from the secret world. Most importantly, the simple answer to the vital question as to whether these agencies, secret or not, are accountable to the democratic process – parliament and the government of the day – is no.

Every year, for instance, a bizarre charade takes place in the Houses of Parliament. Within a matter of minutes, approval is given to the expenditure of many millions of pounds on departments with which the vast majority of MPs have not the slightest acquaintance. In 1979 the figure was £40 million. Its designation is described simply as for the 'foreign and other secret services'. Not for nothing is it colloquially known as The Secret Vote.[1]

Though this annual ritual is one of the rare occasions when the British spying organizations are even mentioned, parliamentary tradition has now ensured that no questions are asked. It is the single exception to the rule that the Public Accounts Committee can inspect the figures. Few MPs believe that the total reflects the real extent of spending, which has been estimated to be more than £100 million for MI5 and MI6 alone.[2]

Questioning the day-to-day operations of the security services has proved equally difficult. Among a long list of ninety-five subjects on which parliamentary questions will not be accepted are 'security operations' and 'telephone-tapping'. When MPs *have* managed to break through this net, they have been given a Ministerial answer which oscillates round the theme that to say more would endanger the national security. It has been left to the rare occasion of a spy defection or a major security leak for any more detailed probing to be allowed, though even during the Anthony Blunt scandal of 1979 the government was hardly forthcoming. Periodic investigations of such scandals have led to little fundamental analysis of the security services' role.

And if our elected representatives remain ignorant, what of the politicians who nominally control the secret agencies? On paper, the Director-General of MI6 is responsible to the Foreign Office, MI5 comes under the Home Office and the Special Branch, as police officers, are controlled by local police committees or, in London, the Home Secretary. Yet the extent to which this apparently straightforward chain of command allows real political control is open to some doubt.

As far as MI6, MI5 and the three armed forces are concerned, a complicated series of committees acts as a filter between the intelligence-gathering agencies and the politicians. Central to these is the Defence Intelligence Committee, which is supposed to supply Ministers with both short- and long-term assessments.

1. According to the 1782 Civil Service List and Secret Service Money Act, the government was limited to spending £10,000 a year on its Secret Service. This law was only repealed, belatedly, in 1977.
2. *New Statesman*, 8.2.80.

There is also a Cabinet Coordinator of Intelligence and Security, whose job is to present reports to the Prime Minister personally. But the suggestion that this system permits genuine two-way access between government and the secret services is belied by other evidence.

A former naval intelligence officer, Donald McLachlan, noted in the *Daily Telegraph* in 1968 that he was surprised to learn from both an ex-Foreign Secretary and his top civil servant that 'they knew next to nothing of the organization and assessment of secret intelligence for which some years ago they had been responsible'. More fundamentally, the only published official instructions to the head of MI5, issued in a terse six-paragraph statement by the Home Secretary in 1952, say specifically that he should not pass on detailed reports to Ministers, only 'such information as may be necessary for the determination of any issue on which guidance is sought'.

The most recent evidence for this distancing of the politicians came in 1979, during the Anthony Blunt scandal. Blunt, a former top MI5 officer, had admitted spying for the Russians, been granted immunity from prosecution in 1964 and then progressed through the establishment to become the knighted Surveyor of the Queen's Pictures. His cover was blown only by a thinly disguised description of his activities in a book on espionage.[1] But though Blunt was in fact the 'fourth man' in a vital chain of spies, a succession of Prime Ministers candidly admitted when the scandal broke that they had no knowledge of the 1964 deal, only subsequently being pushed into reviving their memories. As one former Home Office Minister, Alex Lyon, put it succinctly: 'No politicians know very much about the secret services'.

It would be wrong to assume, however, that there is no contact at all between politicians and the secret agencies. Some examples have already been given, and the Home Secretary does receive regular reports from MI5 about, for instance, 'undesirable aliens'. A number of such cases occur every year, and the Minister's rubber stamp is necessary to put the security service's recommendations into effect. It was a report of this type which eventually led to the deportation of Philip Agee and

1. *The Climate of Treason* by Andrew Boyle (Hutchinson, 1979).

Mark Hosenball, and indirectly to my own tangle with security. How much the Home Secretary is told, how many of the details are fudged, refined or excised, how able he is to cross-examine his sources on their evidence, is far less certain. Similarly, the Attorney-General, Sam Silkin, who approved the ABC prosecution, must have been persuaded by his security advisers that there was a substantial case to answer. In the light of subsequent events, it would appear that this advice was wilfully exaggerated.

It is, after all, the job of the security services to encourage deceit. They can provide false information either because of their own vested interests or because they believe that is what their political masters want to hear. Both MI5 and MI6 were involved in the distribution of the notorious 'Zinoviev letter', a classic red scare forgery which led to the downfall of the 1924 Labour government. At the same time, against a background of criticism of MI5, its first head, Vernon Kell, was said to have retired; in fact he did not do so for a further sixteen years. The technical change in responsibility for the Security Service from the Prime Minister to the Home Secretary, agreed in 1952, was also not revealed to the public for a decade afterwards.[1]

This subterfuge extends even to the names of the Director-Generals of both MI5 and MI6. Listed occasionally in the New Year's Honours List, they are described obscurely as, for example, 'lately attached to MoD'. Their identities are not only covered by D-Notices, a system of restrictions on press reporting of security matters (see Chapter 3), but when both men retired simultaneously in 1977 a special letter was sent to all national newspapers warning against naming their replacements.[2]

In practice, the national press's general acceptance of the conventional silence has left it to overseas publications, or less fearful ones in this country, to break the news already known to most foreign intelligence services. The truth is, as Geoffrey MacDermott, a former Foreign Office adviser to MI6, pointed out: 'The identity of almost all of the senior members of the service is known to the KGB.'[3] It is an equally sobering thought

1. In Lord Denning's Report, 1963.
2. Published in the *Morning Star*, 22.4.78.
3. In *The New Diplomacy* (Plume Press, 1973).

that in both the Soviet Union and the United States the names of the security chiefs are public knowledge.

By contrast with MI5 and MI6, however, the Special Branch should be the most public of the national security organizations. They are, as successive Home Secretaries have been fond of pointing out, only ordinary policemen and -women doing a particularly sensitive job. They should therefore be accountable to their respective Chief Constables just like any other officers, and subject to the usual complaints procedure. In practice they have considerable autonomy, both within the police force itself, and from the Home Office which lays down general guidelines for their work.

Until 1978, few of the forty-odd police authorities in mainland Britain even admitted the existence of the Special Branch. In that year, presumably as a result of a national directive, brief references began to appear in their annual reports. James Anderton, the Chief Constable of Greater Manchester, said the inclusion of a description was 'to dispel silly speculation and doubt'. But the decision to include such information was almost certainly related to increasing public concern about the Branch's activities. By law, Chief Constables have the right to refuse to supply reports to their respective police authorities 'if it would contain information which in the public interest ought not to be disclosed'.

Attempts to take up both general and specific complaints about the Special Branch in parliament have produced uniformly bland responses. Home Secretary Merlyn Rees, for instance, said that he knew a number of Branch officers personally, was protected by them daily and had every confidence in their ability. 'Mistakes are sometimes made,' he added apologetically. 'Perhaps this is inevitable in any area of human activity. Enthusiasm sometimes overcomes what should have been better judgement.'[1]

What might happen were the covers really to be lifted can only be deduced from the experience of Australia. In 1978, the South Australian Special Branch was actually disbanded, nearly all its files destroyed and its chief officer sacked after an investigation

1. House of Commons, 24.5.78.

had found the Branch's dossiers to be 'scandalously inaccurate, irrelevant to security purposes and outrageously unfair to hundreds, perhaps thousands of loyal and worthy citizens'.

During the investigation, carried out by a senior judge on the instructions of South Australian Premier Don Dunstan, a strongroom full of records was inspected at police headquarters. These records included all the South Australian Labour Party politicians (both local and national representatives), half the judges of the Supreme Court, most prominent union officials, homosexuals, members of conservation groups, prominent clergymen in the peace movement as well as thousands of others who had taken part in political activity. There were notes on speeches, photographs and an 'election' file showing evidence of surveillance of MPs.

At the end of the exercise, the judge commented that the files were based 'on the unreasoned assumption that any persons who thought or acted less conservatively than suited the security forces were likely to be potential dangers to the security of the state!'[1] Dunstan himself accused the Special Branch of 'infringing basic civil liberties and engaging in political surveillance of a most biased kind'.

The Police Commissioner for South Australia, Harold Salisbury, was eventually dismissed for repeatedly misleading the State government over what the Branch was doing. Salisbury said in his own defence that he had withheld information intentionally because his duty was to the law, and not to any politically elected government.

The parallels with this country are too close for comfort. The British police are also ultimately responsible to the law, and not to politicians. Historically, the Australian security system was actually set up in 1949 by a former head of MI5, and Salisbury himself was previously Chief Constable of the North and East Ridings of Yorkshire. It is only reasonable to assume that the British practice was carried across the water.

So far, demands for such an inquiry in Britain have met with little success. At the time of the Australian disclosures, the then

1. *Special Branch Security Records*, report by Judge White (Adelaide, 12.77).

Energy Secretary Tony Benn suggested a number of ways in which the security services could easily provide more information about their activities, including staffing, budgets and the number of dossiers kept. More recently, Labour MP Robin Cook has proposed a new law under which MI5 would present an annual report to parliament. The present Conservative government looks unlikely to follow these leads. Meanwhile, the only independent check is through a body called the Security Commission, whose concern is wholly with whether the security surrounding the agencies is tight enough, not whether it is necessary in the first place.

The dangers of lack of accountability are therefore considerable. Without adequate control, the secret agencies can become self-perpetuating elites with their own policies and their own political judgements, what John Berry called in his speech to the jury at the end of our trial, 'a state within a state'. But it is still wrong to see the politicians themselves as some neutral force to be manipulated through ignorance. In our own case it appears that a mixture of security propaganda and governmental pliability led to its escalation into a major issue. As an intelligence expert, John Bruce Lockhart, himself put it: 'Possibly more follies have been committed in the name of security than in any other governmental activity in a modern state.' I shall now turn to how the ABC 'folly' began – in the everyday practices of the security system.

2

A Tap on the Phone

Chief Superintendent Harry Nicholls straightened his tie, puffed out his chest and stared at the ceiling of Tottenham Magistrates Court. 'I went to Berry's flat as a result of information received,' he said cautiously. From the Special Branch officer in charge of the investigations into our alleged offences under the Official Secrets Act it was intended to say nothing and yet, hopefully, everything that would be demanded.

That was not to be. 'Was the source of that information mechanical or human?' came the carefully-worded follow-up from the defence barrister. Mechanical? Human? Nicholls must have been aware of the implications of either phone-tapping or letter-opening.

Unfortunately he was not allowed to answer. Michael Coombe, the State prosecutor, was on his feet with an objection. 'I don't think this officer has first-hand knowledge,' he argued, 'and since I don't know myself how the information was obtained, I am not conceding for a moment that it wasn't done improperly. But the evidence itself is all properly admitted.' In other words, you can break the rules as long as you come up with the goods. The magistrate agreed to bring this embarrassing exchange to a swift conclusion.

In fact, it had already become apparent that surveillance played a crucial part in the arrst of myself, John Berry and Duncan Campbell. Nicholls of the Special Branch, called in at the last minute to perform the snatch, may not have been involved. But others were. And the suspicion that the whole operation was masterminded by MI5, which has responsibility both for long-term surveillance and offences under the Official Secrets Act, remains strong.

It was early in 1977, just before our arrest, that a number of strange things began to happen. At that time the argument over the proposed deportation of the Americans Philip Agee and Mark Hosenball was still occupying the headlines.[1] Behind the scenes, telegrams were winging their way backwards and forwards between Washington and London, and in Whitehall there was genuine concern that the affair was causing more trouble than it was worth.

One organization in particular was kicking up a fuss – the hastily-convened Agee–Hosenball Defence Committee based at the offices of the National Council for Civil Liberties in Kings Cross. The Committee may have been perfectly public, may have used the accepted channels of protest, may have had the support of MPs and other public figures, but that was no reason to exclude it from the lists of the secret snoopers. If anything could be dug up to support an unpopular decision, it was worth having.

For the volunteer workers at the NCCL, the first indication that something was amiss came in January, when two of their address books went missing. One in fact turned up later, and in the rush it seemed much easier to put the disappearance down to carelessness rather than anything more sinister. In practice, as already suggested, lists of addresses are exactly what somebody wanting to check out an organization would look for.

But on 7 February, just ten days before our arrest, something considerably more unusual occurred. That evening, the Committee's treasurer parked her Ford Anglia car in a dimly lit mews in North West London. Inside were a number of documents relating to the Committee's accounts, as well as personal belongings. After just over two hours she returned to find that the quarter-light on the driver's side had been forced, and the contents rifled.

The loss to the Committee was irritating but not vital. Gone was its paying-in book, which showed what had been deposited with the bank. Gone was an account book showing the up-to-date state of its finances. Gone also was a cheque book, which gave clear details of who had been paid for printing posters, leaflets and so on. All useful, of course, to someone whose

1. See Chapter 3 for a fuller description of the Agee–Hosenball case.

fantasies told them that such groups depend for their existence on Moscow gold.

What gave the incident its most bizarre note, however, was the sequel to this potentially commonplace act of larceny. Several weeks later, the treasurer was surprised to learn that some of her personal property had been returned anonymously to Barclay's Bank in South Hampstead. Among the items recovered were her diary, a cheque book and a cheque card. The combination of a cheque book and banker's card would have been an obvious temptation to somebody whose interest was financial. Neither had been used. The clear distinction between personal and Committee property made the thief an unusual one indeed.

Other incidents followed. Four days after the treasurer's unexpected visitor, the Committee's convener, Phil Kelly, went to a dance at the London College of Printing in South London. He emerged to find that his car window had been levered open. But there were no documents or papers in the vehicle and only a coat was taken. Soon after our arrest, the treasurer's car was again burgled and its contents sifted through, though nothing was removed.

At the time, these events were not seen as any sort of pattern. Break-ins, especially to cars, are after all common in all big cities. But their conformity to known Special Branch and MI5 practice, and their concentration just before our own arrest, soon made them appear more than coincidence.

The Home Office itself has always denied any such connection. Even after the department belatedly admitted, many months later, that the incidents had all been reported to the police, it said that 'so far no arrest for these offences has been made and it has not been possible to establish a motive'.[1] To the alleged involvement of MI5 the response was even cooler. 'This is a most serious allegation,' Home Secretary Merlyn Rees told an inquiring MP. 'I can assure you that, whatever may have happened in other countries, neither the police nor the security services nor anybody else in this country has authority to commit

1. Home Office Minister Lord Harris in a letter to Robin Cook MP, 29.7.77.

criminal offences.'[1] But what if they were carried out without that authority, without Rees's knowledge?

As we shall see, that was by no means the end of mysterious break-ins. But if those catalogued already appear in retrospect to have been almost deliberately amateurish, intended to act as a warning that 'we're watching you, so look out', then a parallel operation of much less obvious surveillance was under way. This involved both the opening of letters and the tapping of telephones.

After weeks of soul-searching it was on 4 February, just three days before the treasurer's car was first broken into, that John Berry decided to put pen to paper. How he came to that decision will be explained in Chapter 4. But the import of his message was clear. In a letter to the Agee–Hosenball Defence Committee he wrote that he was an ex-member of Britain's covert 'security' organization, was concerned about its operations and would like to 'know of any medium through which this information could be published'.

Unfortunately, the Committee were not the only people to read the letter. Along with all others addressed to the group it was intercepted by the security authorities, who found it of some interest. They were already looking hard for something to give credence to their action over Agee and Hosenball, to confirm their argument that there were more people willing to investigate 'secret' areas – and something which might also deflect attention from a politically embarrassing decision. Here was the answer to their expectations.

Berry had worked for what they considered to be a totally secret operation – Signals Intelligence. He also wanted to talk about his experiences, possibly to journalists. Before long the telephone lines were buzzing between MI5, the Defence Intelligence offices at the Ministry of Defence (where Berry's army record would be kept), and the headquarters of Signals Intelligence, GCHQ in Cheltenham. But it was Berry's own phone which was made the subject of almost immediate tapping.

Meanwhile, the Agee–Hosenball Committee was keen to know

1. Letter to Robin Cook MP, 28.9.77.

more precisely what Berry had to say. A reply was sent to his letter, asking him to come in and see them. A few days later he turned up, on his afternoon off from work, sat down at a type-writer and tapped out a one-page statement of his views.

That 300-word document, seized by the police, has since been copied dozens of times, classified Secret and then de-classified by an over-cautious and confused bureaucracy, and used as vital evidence of a breach of the Official Secrets Act. But at the time, to an inquiring journalist, it was simply the beginning of a good story.

What it said, in terms of hard facts, was sketchy. It talked of the numbers of people employed on Signals Intelligence – put crudely, international electronic eavesdropping. It mentioned close cooperation with the Americans. It also said that govern-ment expenditure on this type of work was concealed by spread-ing it through different departments, and hinted that even the commercial communications of British companies were inter-cepted.

But it was Berry's attitude to his former job, his clear disillusionment with the undercover work, and his argument that the secrecy was merely a sham to conceal an illegal organiza-tion, which immediately attracted my attention. 'It appears to me', he wrote, 'that secrecy is one of the most important keys to power, and the existence of an organization capable of spend-ing vast sums of money in the total absence of public control should do much to dispel any illusion about the democratic nature of our government.' He also mentioned threats and informers as a regular part of the maintenance of secrecy, and ended with a reference to the 'apparatus which could transform Britain into a police state overnight'.

This was strong stuff. But most importantly, it was directly linked to the deportations of Philip Agee and Mark Hosenball. This was what had motivated Berry to break his silence, this was the story which I, like many other reporters, wanted to get to the bottom of; and crucially, it was an article by Hosenball and Duncan Campbell on the very same subject of Signals Intelligence that had so far been the only suggested reason, though never officially confirmed, for Hosenball's exclusion from

Britain. Maybe Berry, however indirectly, could throw some light on that decision.

Two days after I was handed a copy of Berry's statement, the story was given a dramatic boost in news value. The Home Secretary announced in the House of Commons that Agee and Hosenball would *definitely* be deported. He had heard the arguments, listened to the protest, and that was that. There were headlines, and largely adverse comment, in all the national press. As the reporter who had covered the deportation saga, actively supported the Agee–Hosenball Defence Committee and worked with Hosenball at *Time Out* magazine, this was obviously my area. But to the security services this was just the moment, faced with a renewed outcry over the two Americans, when they desperately needed a diversion.

I had already written to John Berry suggesting an interview with *Time Out*. He had in fact tried to phone me, no doubt a first alert to the tappers, but I was out of the office. By this time I had also discussed the idea with Duncan Campbell, whose knowledge of Signals Intelligence would obviously be invaluable. Not having John's phone number, I called round to see him the day after the deportation confirmation. As far as he was concerned, an interview with the two of us was fine.

That evening, final arrangements were made over the phone. We would arrive at 6.30 the following night and take it from there. As the details came out, the call was carefully monitored.

In the late afternoon of 18 February a team of Special Branch officers was hurriedly assembled at New Scotland Yard. Chief Superintendent Harry Nicholls was put in command and given his instructions by Commander Rollo Watts, then head of Branch operations. The haste of this arrangement was confirmed by the fact that one member of the team had only a scrappy piece of paper with the names of the people to be arrested and the alleged offence. Interestingly, the list included Steve Weisman, a journalist who had done no more than discuss the Berry statement on the phone to the NCCL. It was yet another indication of the extent of the surveillance, and of the fact that other forces, outside the Special Branch team, had been at work.

About an hour and a half after the interview started, a fleet of Special Branch cars positioned themselves outside John Berry's flat. There they sat, watching and waiting. At 9.00 a man came out of the house and walked along the road. Where was he going, the officers asked. To the pub, he replied. He clearly knew nothing about the interview. A false alarm. But by soon after 10.00 the mission had been accomplished: a clutch of three more 'subversives' was in the bag.

The authorities have always refused to confirm this version of how we were arrested, and the scenario of letter-opening and tapping has inevitably been based on intelligent deductions from the information available. For instance, only a handful of people actually knew that the interview was taking place, and its timing was only ever discussed on the phone. John Berry also recalled later that a few days before the interview his phone had emitted a single 'ding' in the early morning, when no one was using it. According to experts, this is one sign (because the circuit has to be broken) that a tapping connection is being made, and short of an informer inside *Time Out* magazine or the NCCL it would have needed the intercepted letter to set that tapping in motion. Finally, immediately after our arrest, both *Time Out* and the NCCL were warned anonymously by a Post Office employee that their phones were being monitored.

What *is* certain is that the technology now available to the state is so extensive that there are few areas of an individual's private life that cannot be satisfactorily probed. Though phone-tapping seems the most obvious explanation, it is always possible that a remote listening device, a bug, was present in John Berry's flat. Add to these devices the telephoto lens, the video camera and the capacity of computers to succinctly record for instant retrieval the information gathered, and the picture is, quite literally, complete.

But it is telephone-tapping, the ability to eavesdrop every time someone picks up the receiver for a chat, that most commonly raises the spectre of Big Brother. There are now over 23 million phones in use throughout Britain. As a means of communication the system often leaves much to be desired; as a means of surveillance it is ideal.

Tapping is carried out by all the agencies already mentioned, from the Special Branch to MI6, as well as the ordinary police and the armed forces. To do this usually requires the co-operation of the Post Office, who run the telephone system, and their assistance is regularly given. Only recently, however, has the full extent of this link-up been revealed.

From a comparatively small operation in the 1960s, when 300 telephone lines could be monitored at any one time, the security agencies now have at their disposal a far more sophisticated tapping centre – where at least 1,000 lines can be listened to simultaneously.[1] Known officially as the Equipment Development Division of the Post Office Operational Programming Department, but colloquially as 'Tinkerbell', the centre occupies a five-storey office block in Ebury Bridge Road, Chelsea. So secretive is its round-the-clock work that doors are kept permanently locked, windows covered by opaque white curtains and its address and phone number confusingly located in the City of London.

In order to listen in on calls, the Chelsea centre is directly linked in to the national telephone network. Every week, a list of numbers to be tapped is circulated to individual exchanges and there a Post Office engineer will connect up a particular line to the national centre, returning later to disconnect the tap. Though normally carried out outside office hours, this work is both routine and simple, and few regular Post Office employees have any idea that it is taking place. Only occasionally have there been cases of objections by other staff. Twelve lines at every 'group' exchange in major cities are said to be available for tapping connections.

From local exchanges the tapped lines are in turn connected to Tinkerbell, using a part of the telephone system designed for military communications, and a sophisticated operation for processing the results then takes over. All calls are automatically transferred, via a computer, to multi-track tape-recorders and storage discs: a single recorder can cope with dozens of lines at a time. But the computer is also able to deal with a previously

1. First described in the *New Statesman*, 1.2.80.

irritating problem – the mass of irrelevant information which inevitably flows in.

Using a programmed retrieval system, the computer will set the recording machine in motion only if a particular number, or numbers, has been dialled by the targetted subscriber. Those numbers can be easily selected either by previous tapping or by the use of a printermeter (described on the following page), thus effectively separating out important contacts from personal friends. The tappers have access to a complete list of telephone numbers in the country, together with names and addresses.

Even more dramatic technical advances include the possibility of programming the computer to home in on conversations containing specific words, such as 'strike' or 'demonstration', to identify particular voices on the line and ultimately, though this is denied by some technical experts, to actually print out a recorded conversation automatically. The effectiveness of the latter potential is said, however, to depend on the quality of the line. All these advanced techniques have been developed for the tappers by researchers at Government Communications Head-quarters in Cheltenham (the subject of our interview with John Berry), and make phone-tapping in the 1980s a massively more precise exercise.

To some readers this might seem acceptable if the 'targets' were the future perpetrators of serious crime, such as armed bank robberies. In practice, experienced criminals know they're likely to be tapped, it's not always possible for the police to react fast enough to a crucial telephone arrangement, and tapping is most useful in monitoring the unthinking discussions of the broad range of people described in Chapter 1. Evidence for this comes from the fact that only 100 lines at the Chelsea centre are reserved for the ordinary police; the rest are allocated to the Special Branch, MI5 and MI6. The last two organizations have direct lines to the centre, over which recorded calls can be replayed.

Alongside this system, the Post Office itself also has a number of ways in which it can independently monitor calls – apart from the obvious example of the operator listening in out of interest. These are not technically tapping, in that in most cases no actual recording is made of conversations. But there has been growing doubt about their potential abuse.[1]

A 'printermeter', officially a Meter Check Printer, can record on to a paper tape the details of all numbers dialled, and the time and the duration of calls from any given telephone. The machine can be plugged in quickly, be left for as long as needed and present the information as simply as the check-out at a supermarket. At least 18,000 printermeters are now in use.

According to the Post Office, printermeters are used largely to provide evidence when a customer queries a bill, and are the primitive forerunners of new electronic exchanges which will enable all calls to be listed and made available to subscribers. But their use to the police, and others, in discovering who is regularly in contact with a particular number, is clear.

Equally common is the system of 'service observation', a scheme officially designed to check traffic patterns, forecast growth and ensure the efficiency of automatic exchange equipment. 200,000 calls are monitored by this system each week, employing 600 specially trained observers. Selected lines at every exchange are wired out to larger 'switching centres' where the monitors sit at consoles. The sensitivity of this work is emphasized by the display of the Official Secrets Act on the wall and the rule that the observation rooms are out of bounds to all but authorized personnel. Only three per cent of calls are said to be listened to live, however, and none recorded.

Service observation is claimed by the Post Office to be essential for measuring the quality of the service, and for 'human factors research', the jargon for dialling errors. Yet in the United States such monitoring has been declared unconstitutional without a court order. In Britain, no such permission is legally required.

Whether the Post Office passes on any of this information to the police is supposed to be limited to special circumstances. These include the possibility of fraudulent, malicious or obscene callers, if one side of a conversation agrees or 'in exceptional

1. See, for example, *Rights* (NCCL newspaper), 8.78.

cases with the express authority of a senior officer at Post Office headquarters'. In fact, according to internal instructions on the 'disclosure of information about telephone calls',[1] this process can be bypassed in exceptional cases and permission given much lower down the hierarchy. Informal arrangements include the case of one Special Branch officer, reported in *Rights*, the NCCL newspaper, who was said to have had frequent discussions with a local telephone supervisor in charge of customer accounts. The instructions say wisely that 'in dealing with requests, care should be taken to prevent any impression arising among subscribers generally that information is given as a matter of course, or that calls are listened to by operators.'

By contrast, phone-tapping proper – the extensive eavesdropping on whole conversations such as occurs in the Chelsea centre – is in theory even more carefully controlled. Every tap requires a warrant to be signed by the Home Secretary, a copy of which is then passed on to the officials who will carry out the interception.

The police are supposed to apply for warrants only when other methods of investigation have failed, when they expect a conviction to result and, for people with a previously clean record, if serious crime is involved. MI5 is similarly limited to a major subversive or spying activity likely to injure the national interest. Warrants granted to the police are subject to review every month, those to MI5 every three to six months.[2] But just how these limitations are interpreted, and to what extent warrants are even used, must be viewed in the light of those organizations' considerable independence. Last year, the *New Statesman* reported that the security agencies had 'carte blanche' over tapping, while the *Sunday Times* noted that warrants were granted 'with steadily greater readiness as the reasons progress upwards from crime to intelligence-gathering'. It's certainly hard to imagine how any Minister could find the time to examine every urgent request for a tap.

1. Telecommunications Instructions, 1972.
2. Restrictions described in *The Birkett Report*, 1957, and still officially in force.

Sensitivity about the subject has meant that only twice have official figures been published on the extent of government-approved phone-tapping. In 1955, 231 warrants were said to have been issued to the police, customs officers and MI5 together, and the government report in which they were contained, that of the Birkett Committee, recommended that no figures should be given again. Soon after the revelation of the existence of the Chelsea centre, however, the government updated these records, showing an increase to over 450 warrants by 1979.[1] Unofficial estimates have set the figure far higher, somewhere between 2,000 and 3,000 official taps a year.[2]

Just how extensive phone-tapping *can* become has already been seen in Northern Ireland, a familiar training ground for police and military equipment. Adapting the Post Office system of service observation, the Army at one time installed a mini computer and multi-track tape-recorders to monitor a vast number of calls from Belfast's telephone headquarters. The tapping equipment became so overloaded at one exchange that new subscribers had to be turned away. At the same time, all overseas calls, telegrams and telex messages are liable to be intercepted by Government Communications Headquarters at Cheltenham, or its American equivalent, the National Security Agency, which has a number of bases in this country. Computerization of the British overseas telegram centre has made this surveillance easier, and the right to do it is enshrined in the Official Secrets Act.

Telling that you're one of those singled out for a personal tap poses a more difficult problem. Inevitably, many more people believe it is happening than can prove it, and it is one of those areas where paranoia runs high. Technically, the most difficult time for the tappers is when the recording starts and finishes. A dead line, or a short sharp ding (as John Berry experienced) when the phone is not in use, may indicate that this is happening. During recording itself, however, equipment is available to ensure that no drop in the current can be detected. Wrong numbers, strange sounds and interference are more likely to be

1. In *The Interception of Communications in Great Britain* (1980).
2. *Sunday Times*, 3.2.80.

the quirks of a poor phone service: the last thing an interloper wants is a bad connection.

On a few rare occasions tapping *has* been detected by its victims. Several groups have planned demonstrations at short notice over the phone and turned up to find the police waiting. The most recent example of this was during the 1980 national steel strike when officials at the steel union's headquarters, suspecting that tapping was taking place, arranged a fictitious picket. A police car and two vans arrived at the venue within four minutes.[1] Private calls have also been interrupted by incautious snoopers. In 1969, a member of a local civil liberties group phoning the NCCL's head office heard a voice come on the line to announce 'Recording finished'.[2] During a conversation with a government department in 1950, MP Sir Tufton Beamish was told by a third, anonymous party: 'Please remember that I have been listening to your conversation. Please remember to be more careful in future.' Whether this was the MP's phone or the civil servant's being subjected to a security check is not known.

Other examples of tapping confirmed by inside sources include the offices of the Grunwick strike committee in 1976 and 1977, monitored through the local Harlesden exchange,[3] and the private rooms of the Patriotic Front delegation during negotiations for the independence of Zimbabwe in early 1980.[4] In the latter case, hotel apartments were also bugged. Though MPs are officially excluded from tapping, this is only unless the 'security of the state' (a phrase as broad as it is wide) could be endangered.

In effect, tapping is only limited by the personnel needed to interpret the results. So it will be the centres of political activity, trade union leaders, opinion-makers such as journalists and public figures, government employees and suspected criminals who make up the main targets. Even so, there are few people on the fringes of professional or political activity who can consider themselves immune. After all, it isn't just the person whose phone

1. *The Times*, 4.2.80.
2. The Home Office refused to comment when he complained.
3. *New Statesman*, 1.2.80.
4. *Sunday Times*, 3.2.80.

is tapped, but anyone that calls them, who is potentially 'subversive'.

Given the secrecy that surrounds its operation, is telephone-tapping therefore illegal? The answer, despite only vague references to passing on information from 'transmissions' in the 1969 Post Office Act, is apparently no. But ironically, it took exactly a hundred years from the inauguration of the telephone service for any attempt to be made to test its legality.

James Malone, a Surrey antiques dealer, had believed for some time that his calls were being listened to. But it wasn't until a court case in which he was charged with handling stolen property that he got definite proof. Asking to see one of the police officers' notebooks, he found details from one of his conversations written down. Two days later, the prosecution made the rare admission that tapping *had* taken place.

Having failed to get anywhere with formal complaints – he claimed on one occasion he was told by the police to use a public call box instead – Malone took his case in 1979 to the High Court. His lawyers asserted, among other things, that tapping was an intrusion on his privacy and confidentiality, and basically unlawful. The government took the case seriously enough to request an intervention from its Solicitor-General, Peter Archer.

After eight days of heavy legal argument, Malone lost. The judge announced that tapping could be legally done 'simply because there is nothing to make it unlawful'. Britain is without a Bill of Rights or any legislation guaranteeing privacy, and though Malone's experience involved no element of 'national security', it seems unlikely that such a case would be viewed any more favourably.

Malone has still to test his arguments before the European Court of Human Rights, supported by the judge's comment that the lack of legal safeguards in Britain would be unlikely to meet its requirements. In other European countries court orders are needed to start a tap and in West Germany, for example, both tapping and letter-opening are officially supervised by a board of five MPs, a permanent Commission, and a series of rules, including one which requires subsequent notification to a suspect 'as soon as this will not jeopardize its purpose'. But perhaps the judge's most poignant comment was that telephone-tapping 'is not a subject on which it is possible to feel any pride in English law'; it 'cried out' for legislation, he said. So far, he has not been taken up on his suggestion.

It's not surprising that phone-tapping arouses such concern. The slightest innuendo, casual observation or joke can be taken out of context, misinterpreted or wilfully misused. The direct evidence from taps is never used in court cases, but can form the essential background. The practice itself remains a closed book for public inquiry.

In the ABC case, it wasn't just the manner of our arrest which implied that tapping had taken place. Towards the end of our ordeal, Duncan Campbell decided to take a two-day holiday in France. At the time, it was a condition of his bail that his passport should be surrendered to the police. But that did not preclude a sixty-hour visit to the Continent, for which an identity card can be obtained at Dover. There had never been any suggestion, anyway, that we might abscond and not turn up in court.

When Duncan inadvertently mentioned his plans on the phone, the alarm bells rang. The very next day he was summoned to appear in court 'for clarification of the bail conditions'. Not surprisingly, a clause was added which said he must not leave the United Kingdom, with or without a passport. For all three of us, the knowledge that someone, somewhere, might be listening in made discussions, particularly over legal tactics, a persistently nervous experience.

If phone-tapping brings surveillance into your living-room, then the opening of letters is not far removed. John Berry's letter to the NCCL was just one of thousands inspected every week, resealed and then returned to follow their path through the supposedly confidential postal system.

Many local post offices have a list of names and addresses whose mail is regularly accorded the attention of the letter-openers. These letters and packages are sorted separately and then handed over to members of the Post Office Investigation Branch, a specialist department of several hundred people whose job is also to check on security within the post and telephone service. At larger postal centres the letters are scrutinized, photocopied if interesting, and the copies sent on to the agency which requested the interception. In London, the main letter-opening department, known as the 'Special Section', is at Union House, close to St Paul's Cathedral.

If the correspondence has to be taken to the Branch's headquarters at Euston Tower, it is carried by a special messenger who waits until it has been examined. The originals are then put back into the normal sorting process without noticeable delay. Letters removed from the system for opening, sometimes called 'spivs', are said to have gone 'upstairs', and the Branch is referred to among Post Office staff by the jokingly sinister title of 'the Gestapo'.

A number of methods are available for discovering the contents of letters. They can be placed under an X-ray machine and either cursorily read or photographed if they look interesting. Alternatively, a fibrescope – a flexible plastic rod no thicker than a piece of wire, with a miniature lens fixed to one end – can transmit video signals to a TV camera using the technology of fibre optics. Those parts of the letter nearest the flap can therefore be read without opening it.

When this proves unsatisfactory, or the letter needs to be opened for a full examination, it can be extracted using a pair of long thin pliers which wind it into a tiny cylinder small enough to come out through the sealing flap. Getting it back is more difficult. But the simplest method is merely to undo the bottom, less obvious flap and then reseal it, if necessary using special glues and chemical solvents. Even a slit down the side can be concealed by employing woodpulp that restores the texture of the paper. In extreme cases, where enthusiasm overcomes technology, a sticker can be placed on a badly damaged envelope reading 'Opened in Error'. The introduction of self-sealing envelopes has made the process even simpler. And anyway, how often does the most suspicious person have the time or energy to inspect his or her correspondence for the tell-tale signs?

Not all letter-opening is carried out on behalf of the police and security services. Letters from abroad can be opened by the Customs and Excise looking for 'obscene' publications or the illegal transfer of currency. But there is ample evidence that the system is used widely to find out what individuals or organizations are thinking and planning. In just one of London's seven main postal districts 100 addresses were reported to be monitored during 1972: about half were political groups.[1]

It is invariably only through mistakes or a disaffected Post Office employee that the game is given away. Letters sent to one address can turn up at a completely different destination: they have simply been transposed by mistake. This happened, for instance, in 1973 between a left-wing bookshop, Rising Free, and the Communist Party,[2] and more recently (1979) between a political activist and the NCCL, with which he had no connection. A police officer may phone up to find out about a particular event only the day after details have been sent to members of a group through the post, as happened to the Hampstead Committee of 100 in 1963.[3] In one case the actual form and envelope used to pass on letters to the Investigation Branch was delivered in error to an anarchist magazine, *Freedom*,[4] whilst Peter Hain, the South African who campaigned against the visit of the Springboks cricket team in 1970, was told by a worker at his local sorting office that his mail 'was taken away by two men in plain clothes and returned in time for normal delivery'.

During the writing of *The Technology of Political Control*,[5] the authors received a steady stream of letters and packages that were torn, battered or plastered with sticky tape reading 'Found Open'. When a letter addressed clearly to one of the writers, Carol Ackroyd, at her home was instead posted to a hospital where she *used* to work (a fact mentioned in the letter itself), a

1. *Undercurrents* magazine, No. 7 (1974).
2. *Time Out*, 16.11.73.
3. See *Mail Interception and Telephone Tapping in Britain* (Hampstead Group, Committee of 100), reprinted 1973.
4. *Time Out*, 29.7.72.
5. By Carol Ackroyd, Karen Margolis, Jonathan Rosenhead and Tim Shallice (Penguin, 1977).

complaint was made to the Post Office. The reply said apologetically that it must have been 'sheer coincidence'.[1] Ironically, the book included details on how the authorities open letters and tap phones.

In our own case, one example stands out. The historian Edward Thompson received a letter one day containing documents about the activities of the Special Operations Executive, the wartime spying organization for which Thompson's brother worked. But although the package had been sent by recorded delivery, it was considerably delayed. In addition, one important document was missing.[2] It seemed more than chance that during the previous few months Thompson had become an active campaigner against our prosecution – writing letters and articles and generally causing a fuss. We always assumed that anyone who wrote to the ABC Campaign office would have their correspondence inspected before it reached us.

As with phone-tapping, there is no clear legal basis for opening letters, and the practice has never been tested in the courts. It rests on the same vague wording of the Post Office Act, which talks of 'a requirement to do what is necessary to inform designated persons holding office under the Crown concerning matters and things transmitted, or in course of transmission, by means of postal or telecommunications services . . .' Persons holding office under the Crown would obviously include the Special Branch, MI5 and MI6.

Warrants should also be issued by the Home Secretary for each address, and the same limitations apply as to tapping: that serious crime is involved and other methods have failed. But, as postal workers have confirmed, there is nothing to stop a police officer just going round to his local sorting office and asking to see the mail for a suspect.[3] Few employees would feel strong enough to resist such a request, especially if the 'national security' is mentioned.

By contrast, no warrant at all is needed for the use of either bugs or cameras, and the technical developments in both these

1. *Time Out*, 8.4.77.
2. *Sunday Telegraph*, 12.11.78.
3. See, for instance, the Committee of 100 pamphlet.

areas have been extensive over the past ten years. At a comparatively open level, Special Branch photographers go to meetings, rallies and marches and snap the faces in the crowd. They are often not distinguishable from the expected representatives of the press, though on occasion they have been spotted and photographed themselves. For example, an unknown man seen snapping people on the Grunwick picket line in 1977, and later at an anti-National Front march in East London, was also photographed arriving with members of the Anti-Terrorist Squad (who work closely with the Special Branch) at the scene of a bomb scare in a trade union office.[1] The results of their work can now be quickly processed by electronic enlargers and automatic developing machines at Scotland Yard. Far more secret is the use of a special briefcase with pinholes in the side through which photos can be taken: this is used particularly by MI6.

Video cameras – small, portable and simple to operate – are also increasingly employed both in the detection of ordinary crime, such as pickpocketing, and for general surveillance. They can be either hand-held, supplementing still photography at a public event, or mounted on prominent buildings. In London, fifty-six cameras linked to monitor screens at Scotland Yard look down on many of the city's main thoroughfares. They are said to be used only for traffic control, but a quite separate network of cameras can be switched on for 'public order purposes': this means marches and demonstrations. Cameras are permanently located on such buildings as the National Gallery in Trafalgar Square and the Treasury in Whitehall, keeping over two hundred square miles of the capital in constant view.

At really large public gatherings, the cameras take to the sky – in helicopters. A 'heli-tele' lens mounted outside the body of a helicopter is powerful enough to pick out individual faces whilst flying overhead. Light intensifiers make it equally possible to employ a movie camera at midnight or midday. Secretly, video cameras have been installed by the police inside a juke box at a Hartlepool pub (to catch drug dealers)[2] – when customers

1. *Leveller*, 12.79.
2. *News Line*, 29.9.78.

removed the device and tried to show it to local journalists they were arrested – and in a Hampshire sports centre to arrest petty pilferers. One security firm manufactures a camera which can be concealed in a light-fitting and triggered into action by light or vibration. As the magazine *Police Review* reported in 1977: 'No secret is made of the fact that the police do have the facility to see in the dark, around corners or from great heights or long distances.'

The potential for mass surveillance is clearly there, even if it has not so far been realized. In Northern Ireland, video cameras have become a major method for watching what happens in the streets. It hardly needs to be repeated that the techniques developed in Ulster, such as police riot shields and helmets, have inevitably found their way across the water.

And when the ultimate intrusion of privacy is required, there is always the creepily named 'bug'. A bug is no more than a miniature radio transmitter operating on a fixed frequency with its own microphone and power source. But it is also no longer the preserve of detective fiction. Dozens of companies manufacture bugs for use by anyone from industrial spies wanting to know another company's business secrets to the agencies of national security.

Bugs can be concealed in ashtrays, behind curtains, under a table or in a filing-cabinet. With time, they can be drilled into furniture, a skirting-board or a ventilation system. They can be worn under the disguise of a pen, a watch, cufflinks or a lapel badge. And they can be combined with telephone-tapping by fitting a 'drop-in' transmitter that looks exactly like the conventional phone mouthpiece. Conversations both in a room and over the telephone can then be eavesdropped.

Even the problems of their generally limited range and dependence on batteries can be overcome. Expensive bugs have a listening area of up to a mile. Their battery lifetime can be preserved through switching on and off externally by a signal. They can also take their power from the telephone wires themselves or from the mains electricity via a transformer. The 'infinity bug' allows a snooper to dial a number on his own phone, apologize for the mistake, wait for the receiver to be replaced and then send a special tone over the wires. This activates the bug already placed in the victim's handset and enables listening to a private discussion over a considerable distance.

At the most sophisticated level, conversations can be monitored by sending microwave beams on to a vibrating drum, hidden in an office. The effect of speech rhythms on the drum can eventually be transformed into understandable language. Oscillations set up by talking on the outside windows of buildings can be similarly translated. But these are the methods of the major international spying organizations, such as the CIA and the Russian KGB, though MI5 is also said to have developed a laser monitoring device capable of such feats.

The extent to which the more mundane bugging of offices and homes is used by the police and security agencies is not known. But the Special Branch, MI5 and MI6 reportedly share a joint electronic surveillance and bugging centre in Camberwell, South London – marked out by electrically operated gates and tall radio masts. The Post Office also experiments with bugs at its secretive R12 Special Investigations Division near Ipswich, where 400 bugs were said to have been ordered in one year, whilst the Diplomatic Telecommunications Maintenance Service (linked to GCHQ) provides both bugging and de-bugging equipment for government departments. DTMS officers are said to instal bugs by posing as Post Office engineers and to ensure that no regular telephone engineer follows in their footsteps.[1]

Bugging is obviously most useful when a particular meeting is known to be taking place: even then, as with phone-tapping, a lot of useless information can be picked up. There is also the danger of detection either, as the Watergate buggers found, in the act of installation, or through 'sweeping' by a de-bugging machine. Bugs do not, however, carry any signature as to their origin.

In reality, there is little that can be done, short of constant watchfulness or keeping your mouth shut, to protect the privacy of your communications. Someone who operates a transmitter,

1. These departments were described in the *New Statesman*, 8.2.80.

such as a bug, without the permission of the Post Office is technically liable to prosecution under the Wireless and Telegraph Act. But what if it is done by the Commissioner of Police or the Security Service? And how, anyway, do you prove it? The resulting information can be used indirectly in a court case, whether the law was broken in its collection or not. As our own experience proved, even careful questioning of witnesses is unlikely to expose the secretive techniques of modern technology.

What happens to the results of all these technological methods of surveillance? Even if not used immediately for an arrest or search, they will eventually find their way, along with those from more straightforward inquiries, on to a file. But for file, in the 1980s, read computer.

During the past twenty years computers have revolutionized the collecting of information. They make it possible to store vast amounts of it compactly and scientifically, to retrieve it in an instant, and to cross-check or isolate items in a manner impossible through an ordinary file. No large organization, state or private, is now without its centralized data bank, least of all the police.

At the hub of the police computer system is the mammoth Police National Computer (PNC) located in Hendon, North London. In its first seven years of operation this facility cost over £15 million to develop and run, has a capacity for 40 million individual entries (one for every adult member of the population) and is claimed to be 'the largest data retrieval system of its kind in Europe'. It officially stores information on criminal convictions, stolen vehicles, fingerprints, wanted and missing people as well as millions of vehicle owners in the country – transferred automatically from the licensing centre in Swansea. Directly linked to hundreds of television screens in police stations around Britain, the results of a search through the computer's memory can reach a patrol car or beat officer within seconds. Over 50,000 inquiries pass through it every day.

From the list above it might be assumed that these records are entirely factual, enabling a police officer, for instance, to check whether a car is genuinely owned by the person who claims it. This is far from being true, and the computer contains a substantial amount of comment and 'suspicion'. The very fact that car owners are included, together with their date of birth and address, allows considerable freedom for the police to slot in personal details on individuals they judge to be socially unacceptable.

Evidence of this came to light most dramatically in 1977 when a police patrol checked out a car parked in a service area on the M6 motorway. The PNC record revealed that its owner was 'a prominent member of the Anti-Blood Sports League', a snippet of information which an enterprising officer linked to the desecration of hunting hero John Peel's grave over sixty miles away. Three people were eventually arrested. In fact the owner of the car was treasurer of the Hunt Saboteurs Association, but the incident raised the question as to what other non-criminal activities might be entered on the computer.[1] It also uncovered a number of occasions on which Association members had been stopped, questioned or their car numbers taken down, surveillance which seemed not unconnected with the previous police seizure of the organization's membership list. The Home Office only reluctantly admitted that 'information about association with an organization' *was* kept on the PNC.[2]

Such computerized collection of background intelligence rather than hard fact has in practice become increasingly common, and has reached its most sophisticated form in an experimental system operated by the Thames Valley police force. This centralizes a mass of observation and gossip from local police station 'collators', who in turn get it from officers' notebooks. It includes everything from personal habits to favourite haunts, mostly nothing to do with a particular crime. One example of what can be filed away was a collator's report that a man 'fancied little boys' (an allegation later proved to be untrue) and that another was a 'well-known local druggy'. The danger of such observations becoming 'fact' once on the computer are obvious, and even the magazine *Police Review* described this type of entry as 'unchecked bunkum'. But the system continues to expand towards its eventual aim of monitor-

1. *Datalink*, 24.10.77.
2. House of Commons, 2.12.77.

ing ten per cent of the local population and nearly all vehicles and addresses.

So far, this experiment has not been extended on a national basis, but a number of its elements are already incorporated in one of the most frightening recent developments – the Metropolitan Police criminal intelligence computer. Shrouded in secrecy, this is understood to have started operation during 1978 from a site in Putney, South London.[1] Though also used by other departments, the biggest user of all is the Special Branch: almost half the computer's total capacity of 1.3 million names has been allocated to the Branch, most of whom will come under the vague definition of 'subversive'.

The full extent of Special Branch files is greater even than those on the computer. Seven years ago (1974) they contained over a million names, split into twenty-seven unidentified 'areas of interest', as well as thousands of addresses and phone numbers (presumably connected with interceptions) and several other categories. At that time these files were expanding at the rate of 2,000 new names every month.

Those selected for transfer to the new computerized system will be not only more quickly accessible to an inquirer but liable to its method of multi-factor searches. This allows, for instance, such a sketchy demand as for 'a list of females aged 20–35 working for community groups in Leeds' to be fed in. Since the initial information is itself based on unrelated and frequently unsubstantiated details about people's views and lifestyle, the possibility for surveillance or harassment of large numbers of people is dramatically increased.

The dangers of computerization of such intelligence, particularly that of the Special Branch, are therefore considerable. Quite apart from the suspect reasons for its collection, it can be inaccurate, incomplete, out of date or totally untrue, and yet simply linked up to an alleged crime. At the same time, information given to one organization can easily find its way into the hands of another, as with car ownership records. And once on the machine, the record is unlikely to be erased.

Such concerns have led other European countries, including

1. First revealed in *The Times*, 14.2.77.

France and West Germany, to introduce laws either protecting the public against misuse of computerized information or allowing them to check their entries for accuracy. In Sweden, a Data Inspection Board is specifically allowed to look at all police files, even those on security matters. But in Britain there is still no legislation even generally concerned with personal privacy.

In 1978 a government-sponsored committee recommended the establishment of a Data Protection Authority,[1] whose powers would include the registration of most computers storing personal information and the introduction of a code of practice on how they worked. Although these ideas were by no means revolutionary, and didn't include any right of access to the records themselves, no action has so far resulted.

But the committee's most revealing experience was when it attempted to discover even the most general details about computers used by the Special Branch and MI5. On MI5 it discovered nothing; on the new Metropolitan Police computer no more than it could read in the newspapers, despite 'pressing inquiries'. Both the Home Office and the police maintained that anything to do with police intelligence-gathering or national security should be exempted from either investigation or supervision.

This total refusal to cooperate prompted an unusually angry response from an otherwise cautious body. The committee concluded that, on the Metropolitan Police computer, it could give no assurance that the public need not be alarmed, whilst it described MI5 as existing in 'a hermetic compartment where they can never discuss their problems with anyone outside their own tight community. They are therefore not open to the healthy – and often constructive – criticism and debate which assures for many other public servants that they will not stray beyond their allotted functions.'

That an official government inquiry should have been unable to probe these important areas only emphasized the lack of public accountability of the security services. Yet in the next ten years, computers are likely to further increase their potential

1. Report of the Committee on Data Protection, chaired by Sir Norman Lindop.

for social control. In Northern Ireland, for example, a computer employed by the Army now takes in a third of the entire population, and most of its cars and houses, encompassing such refined details as a person's furniture and wallpaper. Against that background, a universal personal identity system such as an ID card, matched to all the various data banks and allowing far greater scope for surveillance, does not seem so remote a possibility.

I myself now have a record in the Police National Computer. Its reference number is 27949/77F. There will also be a dossier kept by the Special Branch, and the same applies to John Berry and Duncan Campbell. But with the arrest of the three of us under a law as powerful as the Official Secrets Act, the possibility emerged for much more open surveillance than the methods described so far in this chapter.

Any of our friends and contacts could be quite openly investigated under the blanket of 'further inquiries'. Altogether in succeeding months, over a hundred people were questioned by the police. Some of these were later to be prosecution witnesses, and some had a purely incidental connection, such as the shop where my tape-recorder was bought. But for a number of people the arrival of the Special Branch was a frightening experience they are unlikely to forget.

Even so, as I have already indicated, the events of 18 February did not bring to an end the series of 'undercover operations'. Cars were regularly parked outside the houses of friends and legal advisers, the occupants leafing endlessly through copies of the *Daily Telegraph*. When approached, they pretended to be embarrassed, claimed no connection with the police and wound up their windows. After John Berry's release from prison, the same driver arrived every morning outside my own home for three days, until I asked him politely to move on. Were they really waiting for a Russian spy, or just causing a nuisance?

And the mysterious visits continued. A week after our arrest a friend, Roger Protz, who had handed in a message at Muswell Hill police station, noticed a strange yellow cross on one of his car windows. Not only did it refuse to come off when he took the vehicle through an automatic car-wash, but a few days later the very same window was used for a break-in. A briefcase was stolen. When this was returned some time later, reported found in a front garden, a cheque book inside was unused. Perhaps sadly for the thief, it contained no details of the ABC case.

Two months later another supporter of the growing campaign against our prosecution, journalist Aidan White, had a similar experience. Whilst away at a conference his flat was burgled, but though drawers were opened and papers scattered, nothing of value – not even a radio, TV, camera or loose change – was taken. Even the local police had to admit that the intruder must have been searching for something.

Whatever that was, the only obvious link between these two incidents was that both victims were active in the National Union of Journalists, an organization whose influence on our case was clearly important. To discover in advance what the union was planning would be useful 'intelligence'. It was also an early sign that we were up against forces which would stop at nothing to muddy the waters.

At the same time, the Special Branch began to look round more openly for evidence to support its contention that the ABC trio were 'a threat to the security of the state'. That its efforts were concentrated on the associates of Duncan Campbell was no coincidence.

Duncan had written extensively about sensitive subjects – computers, defence, bugging, surveillance – as well as a whole range of technical and scientific matters. He was, and is, an expert in communications. His skill has been to probe behind the bland press release and explain complicated technical details in a language everyone could understand. He had added two and two together and made four, not the five which the authorities would have him believe. He was a walking example of exactly the sort of investigative journalism the state was learning to dislike, and with the removal of Duncan's entire research material – books, files, letters and notes – from his Brighton flat, the opportunity was there to chart his vast range of contacts. All that was needed was to follow them up.

Though none of the resulting visits had the full horror of the treatment accorded some people, especially political groups and members of the Irish community following a terrorist bomb, their intention was similar. Not one of Duncan's contacts was ever charged with a criminal offence. But if they could be told in no uncertain terms that they were treading on dangerous ground, and if the impression was created that a far larger conspiracy existed, then that was justification enough.

At Lancaster, for instance, postgraduate student Steven Wright was woken one morning by the arrival of six Special Branch officers in his front room. His cooperation in a thorough search was encouraged by the threat that they would make their presence 'obvious' to neighbours. In fact this had already happened and the local police called, only to be told it was all 'official'.

Having gathered up large bundles of papers, letters, diaries and photographs, the team then took Wright to Lancaster University, where he studied. Informed that 'academic freedom' was at stake, the officer in charge, Detective Chief Inspector Malcolm Moffat (also involved in our arrest), replied that this was a matter of national security, and doors would if necessary be broken down to get what he wanted. A search of Wright's college room produced nothing. After further questioning for over five hours at a police station, Wright was told he could face prosecution under the Official Secrets Act. He was given 'police bail', a system by which there is no need to go to a magistrates court, and told to report back in a month.

Wright's heavy-handed treatment produced an immediate outcry both at the university and nationally. An MP, Robin Cook, described it as 'quite deliberate harassment'. Lancaster's Vice-Chancellor, Charles Carter, issued a statement saying that 'those who work in universities cannot expect to be exempted from the law. But they can reasonably ask for sympathetic understanding of their duty to seek access to all evidence relevant to their studies. Truth is not something to be determined by the state.'

What had Steven Wright done? Little more than write to Duncan Campbell asking for information, borrow some files and take a photo of his local Post Office tower. Such photos were produced unsuccessfully as evidence against Duncan at our eventual trial. Equally relevant may be the fact that his research was into the police's own use of technology. But after threatening legal action to ensure the return of his vital research documents, Wright waited nervously to be prosecuted. It never happened.

Other approaches to Duncan's correspondents were, by comparison, bizarre. Writer Edward Cookridge, himself a former member of MI6, so confused his Special Branch visitors that they promised never to return. A Christmas card sent by a university friend was photocopied and its author questioned on its significance. 'Hi, Duncan. Have not seen you for a long time', it read, as indeed he hadn't. A lorry-driver neighbour was told that the manuscript of his life story would be kept by the police 'for several months'.

For one man, however, the arrival of the Branch meant the immediate loss of his job. Following a visit by both police officers and a member of the Post Office Investigation Branch, an engineering research officer who knew Duncan was suspended from work for suspected 'disclosure of information'. He got no pay, no compensation and no right of appeal. Several months later, after a search of his parents' home, hours of interviews and the constant threat of the Official Secrets Act, the man's only offence was said to be against internal Post Office regulations. He had taken home a copy of the office phone directory. He never got his job back.

The disruptive effect of these investigations proved two-edged. To some people it only emphasized the seriousness of the original arrests. To others it underlined the authorities' desperate need to bolster a weak case, and added to the ranks of our supporters and sympathizers. But the most important escalation in the ABC affair came over three months after our conversation in John Berry's flat.

In May 1977 we returned to Tottenham Magistrates Court for the seventh time. We had been waiting patiently for the Attorney-General, Sam Silkin, to make up his mind whether to approve the continued prosecution – a necessary procedure in all Official Secrets cases. We half expected the whole thing to be quietly dropped. In fact, exactly the opposite happened. Not only did

3

Transatlantic Passage

It should now be clear that the ABC case was being treated with considerable seriousness. The Special Branch, the outward arm of the security services, and almost certainly MI5, had pursued their investigations with the persistence of ferrets after a prey. Phones had been tapped, letters opened, friends and acquaintances watched, dozens of people interviewed or harassed. It was easy to laugh at their occasional mistakes, but the results were hardly amusing. The Attorney-General had been persuaded to give his approval to one of the most powerful charges on the statute book. Never before had journalists been accused of what amounted to spying.

For the three of us, the depression which followed this development was immense. John Berry in particular faced a heavy gaol sentence if found guilty. We had already decided to stick together and fight whatever the law could muster against us, but this was the severest test so far. Even some of those who had been sympathetic to our treatment under the lesser charges now began to have their doubts, and a protest poster which appeared at the time only emphasized the absurd reality. 'These three people spent an evening talking together', it read above our photographs. 'They could now go to prison for fourteen years.'

But it was equally clear that we were not being accorded the status of 'enemies of the state' just because of what we ourselves had done. An interview between two reporters and a Corporal who left the Army seven years before might well have acquired great significance to the proprietors of the secret world. Yet it also represented much more than that.

The fear which underlay much of this extraordinary effort against the ABC trio was one of sheer questioning and exposure. Journalists could not be allowed to use the 'freedom of the press' to investigate how the state carried out its national security surveillance. We had lifted only a small corner of the veil of secrecy, but others, encouraged by our example, might well want to know more. John Berry himself had talked at the interview about a 'snowball effect'. And if there was one country to which the British security system looked with horror, it was the United States of America.

In the two years immediately before our arrest the American agencies of national security had been subjected to a series of official inquiries unprecedented in their history. Every aspect of their secret work had been probed and analysed. Their senior officials were questioned, their agents cross-examined. For the American public this was its first opportunity to hear from the horse's mouth what had been done in its name. But in the corridors of Whitehall this was exactly the type of examination which was feared, and is still feared, most.

Why this happened as dramatically as it did has much to do with the American political and social system. Whereas in Britain Members of Parliament are elected and in turn form a government, in the United States there is a clear separation between the executive and the elected representatives. Though the President himself is elected, the advisers who form his 'Cabinet' are not. The efficient working of the system is therefore crucially dependent on the confidence of the American people – and their representatives in Congress – in the man they vote for as President.

That confidence had been severely undermined in recent years. The protracted war in Vietnam, with its heavy cost in both lives and money, had made Americans think long and hard about their country's foreign policy. The emerging scandal of Watergate had shown not only the fundamental corruption of the political system, but that a President himself could lie. Both issues were in different ways connected to the policies and methods of national security.

At the same time the American press, less trammelled by restrictions than its British counterpart, had begun to home in on the abuses of the security services. When the *New York Times* revealed in December 1974 that the CIA, supposedly restricted to overseas activities, had been involved in surveillance of protest groups *within* the United States, the dam finally burst. The President attempted to hush up the affair, Congress decided to act.

Using powers inconceivable in the House of Commons, Congress was able to demand the appearance of any public official, at whatever level, and to inspect secret documents. From its initial inquiries the investigation fanned out: as one door into the secret world was opened, it only exposed another locked compartment. Revelation followed revelation, and altogether, between 1974 and 1976, a series of official inquiries produced over 2,000 pages of reports.[1] All of these were eventually made public, and what emerged made chilling reading.

To start with, the total cost of the United States intelligence agencies was estimated to be over 10 billion dollars a year, considerably more than had ever been suggested before. One inquiry concluded that the true figure might be twice as much. And though much of this was said to be spent on technological spying – satellites, electronic listening and other methods – it was the activities of the Central Intelligence Agency, the CIA, which attracted the most concern.

For the first time, the CIA was shown through its own records to have systematically violated the human rights and democratic institutions of other countries. In a series of undercover operations spanning more than twenty-five years it had regularly interfered with elections, manipulated coups, spread false propaganda, financed secret armies, bribed politicians and supported the most brutal dictatorships. All in the name of the national security of the United States.

In country after country – ally and enemy alike – the Agency had established its network of agents, including government officials, journalists, union leaders and company executives. Through these chosen individuals it was able to indirectly penetrate every conceivable area of public and private life, and through them its secret programmes were carried out.

1. Notably the Rockefeller Commission, the Pike Report (of the House of Representatives) and the Church Committee, from whose reports the following examples are taken. A summary of their findings is contained in Philip Agee's introduction to *Dirty Work: The CIA in Western Europe* (Lyle Stuart, 1978).

The network was also supported by a vast range of 'proprietories', or CIA-owned companies. They included airlines, training schools for foreign police and military officials, radio stations such as Radio Free Europe, newspapers and publishers. The Agency's propaganda machine was so large that at one time it controlled over 230 news services around the world. Hundreds of books had been published by the CIA without ever identifying its involvement, and in some cases its own fabricated stories had been picked up from abroad and reprinted, as though true, in the American national press.

But the purpose of this international network was not just to wage a war of words. From its origins as a defensive measure to counter communist subversion after the Second World War, the CIA had quickly become an offensive, and secret, instrument of American foreign policy. Its largest and most important department, Clandestine Services, had grown to specialize in what the Agency called 'covert action' – direct intervention in the politics and economy of other countries. The philosophy of covert action was that any method, whether legal under United States law or not, could be used to further its ends, and when the country's policy-makers wanted to intervene secretly in another nation's affairs it was to the CIA that they turned.

During the course of the Congressional investigations many hundreds of these covert action operations were examined. For example, in just one South American country, Chile, the CIA had spent over thirteen million dollars in its efforts to undermine the election, and eventual government, of Salvador Allende's socialist party. It had financed, and then planted stories in, the main newspaper chain, it had supported a crucial lorry drivers' strike and it had encouraged the assassination of General Rene Schneider, Commander of the Chilean Army, in order to provoke a coup. At one point it assisted in the spending of hundreds of thousands of dollars by the multinational ITT corporation in opposition to the socialist party's election. Its reward was Allende's murder during a military take-over and his replacement by a dictatorship whose trademark has been brutality.

Around the world there seemed scarcely any movement against radical change that had not at some stage received CIA backing. In Italy it had supplied millions of dollars towards the election campaigns of the conservative Christian Democrats. Against Cuba it had planned the ill-fated 'Bay of Pigs' invasion. In Australia it had infiltrated the trade unions in order to disarm potential militants. In Greece it had supported the now deposed regime of Colonel Papadopolous and in Laos, for over a decade, it had directed a secret army of thousands of mercenaries in a conflict ultimately as disastrous as that in Vietnam.

One single operation summed up the sheer cynicism of the CIA's covert action policy. At the request of the Shah of Iran, a close American ally, it had begun in 1972 to channel sixteen million dollars' worth of aid to the movement for autonomy in Kurdistan. The Kurds were then, as now, claiming territory on either side of the border between Iran and neighbouring Iraq. But to the Shah, who was in dispute with the Iraqis over another part of that same border, the Kurdish rebellion was simply a useful element to be exploited.

The CIA's generosity did not last, however. When the border dispute was settled three years later, the secret financing was also immediately halted. For the Kurds this was literally disastrous: the Iraqis advanced in a bitter search and destroy operation, crushing the Kurdish movement and leaving 200,000 refugees. In response to pleas for humanitarian assistance, the American response was simple. As a senior official himself explained to a Congressional Committee: 'Covert action should not be confused with missionary work.'

And when such methods failed, there was always the ultimate sanction of assassination. In 1975, a special committee of the United States Senate investigated five alleged assassination attempts by the CIA against foreign politicians, involving, among others, Fidel Castro. Though no evidence was found that the Agency had been successful, it was more than coincidence that four out of the five had in fact been murdered. That Castro alone survived was in itself surprising: during eight plots to kill the Cuban leader the proposed methods had ranged from poison pens to deadly bacterial powders to a cigar impregnated with a toxic chemical.

These crude attempts to further American interests abroad

inevitably shocked the investigators, but they were equally surprised to learn that the CIA had not ignored potential 'targets' much closer to home. Ever since its creation the Agency was shown to have been carrying out covert action operations against United States citizens in direct violation of both its charter and the laws of the country.

The techniques employed were those familiar from the British organizations, only on a far larger scale. The CIA's mail-opening programme, for example, had resulted over a twenty-year period in the inspection of more than 28 million items, the photography of almost 3 million letters and the direct opening of 215,000 pieces of correspondence. At the same time, phones were tapped, offices and homes burgled and political organizations infiltrated. The Agency's domestic filing system was so extensive that it even contained the names of 300,000 people who had been arrested for offences relating to homo-sexuality.

The CIA also instigated a series of horrific experiments in the control of human behaviour. Drugs, hypnosis, electric shocks and sensory deprivation had all been used to discover how information could be extracted under pressure. Hundreds of unwitting victims were subjected to these methods, including mental patients, prisoners and people selected at random off the streets. On one occasion a man had committed suicide after the drug LSD had been administered surreptitiously in his drink.

But not only the CIA was involved in this extensive incursion into Americans' civil rights. Whilst the Agency had its Operation Chaos, aimed at monitoring and disarming the protest movement over the Vietnam war, the Federal Bureau of Investigation had its Cointelpro programme, through which dozens of radical groups were targeted for surveillance and disruption. During 1976 the FBI spent twice as much on informers against 'subver-sive' organizations as it did against organized crime. Meanwhile, the National Security Agency, the technological spying organiza-tion, had intercepted millions of private telegrams, while the Army's own intelligence service had amassed files on thousands of individuals. These encompassed, according to one official report, 'virtually every group seeking peaceful change in the United States'.

Altogether, it was a grim catalogue of what soon became known as the 'crimes' of the American intelligence services, and its effect is still being felt. If one organization now represents to millions of people the fear that they will be spied on, manipulated, bugged or bribed, it is the Central Intelligence Agency. Yet it was also clear that these operations were not aberrations of a bureaucracy out of control. They were an integral part of American foreign and domestic policies, and in many cases they had been directly approved by the President himself and his closest advisers.

Partly for this reason, the result of the unique series of revelations between 1974 and 1976 was not as dramatic as might have been expected. Although the CIA's morale and prestige were badly dented – and there have been considerable internal ructions – the Agency did not collapse overnight. The investigators themselves were highly critical of individual operations, but these were only crudely classified into 'successes' and 'failures'.

Surveillance inside the United States was uniformly condemned, as was the assassination programme. The Chilean venture was considered a failure only because it 'did not command public approval', not for its effect on the people of the country itself. Others were labelled unsuccessful because of the waste of resources and money. But there was little fundamental criticism of the basic tenets of national security on which all these activities had been based.

Even so, it would be wrong to minimize the effect of those investigations. In America they strongly encouraged the spirit of inquiry that had launched them in the first place. There are now numerous organizations concerned to monitor the security services and work towards their reform. Using the Freedom of Information Act, under which the contents of official files can be divulged, they have been able to discover even more about the workings of American national security – and occasionally about British 'secrets'.

At the same time, it was inevitable that the suspicion aroused over the CIA's covert action policy would filter across the

Atlantic. After all, the Agency owed its very origin to the expertise of the British Secret Service. According to one former State Department official, John Marks, the CIA never did anything between 1947 and 1954 'without British approval and help. We learned our dirty tricks from the British, who were so much better at it.'[1] So, if the techniques had been basically the same, what had the Special Branch, MI5 and MI6 been up to since the beginning of the Cold War?

But the attitude of the British authorities was equally predictable. They had already shown their colours in response to one Congressional committee's request for information on the interception of telegrams. The official reply was: 'It is not in accordance with Her Majesty's Government's policy to comment on such matters.'[2] That determination not to tolerate any similar inquiries in this country soon displayed itself against two individuals in particular: two Americans with the unlikely names of Philip Agee and Mark Hosenball.

Philip Agee was thirty-seven when he came to live in Britain in 1972. From his family background he should by then have been well settled into a secure, professional career: a lawyer, maybe, or a businessman. In fact his chosen path lay elsewhere. For twelve years he had been a secret operations officer with the CIA, a job which he increasingly came to hate.

Originally plucked from his upper-crust university by a busy recruiter, Agee at first believed implicitly in 'The Company', as the CIA is known to insiders. His task, in his own words, was to be 'a warrior against communist erosion of freedom and personal liberties around the world, a patriot dedicated to the preservation of my country and our way of life'. Part of his training was a series of interrogations, including a lie detector test, intended both to judge his reliability and to emphasize that secrecy about his work must be 'permanent, eternal and universal'.

In the field, Agee soon discovered what much of the secrecy was about. Under the cover of a succession of South American

1. Quoted in the *Guardian*, 8.12.76.
2. *The Times*, 28.9.76.

embassies he was directly involved in the type of covert action operations for which the CIA has since become infamous. Spies were recruited to infiltrate political parties, forged documents planted to discredit politicians, elections rigged, fake newspapers produced and government officials regularly bribed. Any movement for radical change was penetrated and disrupted.

But while others accepted their role, Agee began gradually to question it. He had been told that the purpose of American foreign policy in Latin America, of which the CIA formed a secret part, was to promote social and economic reforms. Yet the result of his work appeared to be exactly the opposite. By propping up supposedly 'friendly' political forces the CIA ensured only that an ill-educated peasant population remained subservient to oppressive regimes. It wasn't as dramatic as the CIA-backed coup in Chile, but it was still a frightening example of how reform and social change could be quashed.

Eventually, Agee's growing political awareness and mounting disillusionment led him to one inescapable conclusion: he must get out. Using the excuse of personal problems (he had recently been divorced), he resigned. But soon after leaving he came to an even more important decision. He would put his ideas and experiences on the record.

This was a particularly brave and dangerous step. Even if he wasn't prosecuted, a more difficult process than under the British Official Secrets Act, the CIA would undoubtedly do all it could to disrupt his efforts. His book, eventually published in 1975,[1] would be the first ever diary of the CIA's field operations – and included a long appendix of named agents and their contacts. It was unlikely to go down well with The Company.

In fact, right from the point of his departure from the closed community of covert operations, Agee realized he was a marked man. Whilst working on his book in Paris he was visited by an ex-colleague who quietly warned him of the Agency's displeasure. Surveillance by the French security authorities, presumably working at the CIA's behest, forced him to live at a secret address. Even a 'friend' who helped him out with money

1. *Inside the Company: A CIA Diary* (Penguin).

turned out to be a CIA agent. At one stage she presented him with an ingeniously sinister gift, a bugged typewriter.

Once in England, where Agee used the British Museum's library of newspapers to complete his diary, the surveillance still continued. But with his book in print and with this country's reputation for sympathy towards political refugees, he felt more relaxed. He carried on with his exposures of CIA activities around the world, becoming something of a guru to those who wanted to follow a similar path; among those who were infected by this pursuit of the intelligence agencies was Mark Hosenball.

Hosenball came to investigative writing by a completely different route. At twenty-five, he was the son of the chief legal adviser to the US National Aeronautics and Space Administration (NASA). He first crossed the Atlantic to go to secondary school and later to university in Dublin. But as his interest in studying waned, so he turned to journalism for a living. For three years, from 1973, he was one of a trio of reporters, including myself, in the newsroom of *Time Out* magazine.

Time Out has always been an odd mixture of weekly entertainment guide and radical politics. Every week it provides detailed information on hundreds of London events – films, theatre, rock music, art exhibitions, ballet, sport, kids' shows and so on – a formula that has proved an enormous commercial success. Started with just seventy pounds in 1968, it now sells over 70,000 copies. But it has also concentrated on the off-beat and the anti-establishment, and the news department in particular has established a reputation for digging up sensational, and embarrassing, stories. It was *Time Out*, for instance, which first exposed the saga of the Littlejohn brothers and their connection with MI6.

What Mark Hosenball brought to the magazine was a flair for in-depth investigation. Surrounded by piles of newspaper cuttings and notes, he would sit for ages puffing at cigarettes and then suddenly burst into action. At times, all the phones in the cramped and dingy Kings Cross office would be waiting for calls from his contacts. The results were often dramatic, but it was his stories on the involvement of the CIA in Britain which caused the biggest stir.

Like other reporters, Hosenball had read with interest the American revelations about the Agency's international activities. Why, they asked, shouldn't it be happening here? Using a system of checking the list of accredited diplomats to the United States Embassy in London, it was possible to isolate those working under cover, for example as 'political liaison officers', with the CIA. Over fifty CIA officers employed at the Embassy were eventually named in *Time Out*,[1] and their organization described.

Finding out what the CIA was actually doing in Britain proved more difficult. But articles followed about its secret funding of numerous groups concerned with European economic and political cooperation and, most spectacularly, a London-based news agency, Forum World Features.[2] Forum had been carefully set up to push out anti-Communist propaganda, it folded suddenly just before the *Time Out* article and it was run, according to the CIA itself, 'with the knowledge and co-operation of British Intelligence'.

Such stories did not gain quite the national publicity Hosenball might have expected. A natural caution towards the 'fringe' journalism of *Time Out* was coupled with a deep-rooted respect for the transatlantic alliance. One national daily paper refused to publish the names of the CIA agents in London on the basis that the Americans were 'our friends'. At the same time, investigative journalism had not taken off enough in Britain for a small magazine to devote the necessary resources.

Somewhat disillusioned, Hosenball left to join the *Evening Standard*, a conservative and respectable bunker from which he could make sallies into the Fleet Street morning dailies. He wrote about magicians, local councils and plane crashes, nothing in the slightest bit controversial. And if there was one person he thought least about, it was Philip Agee, a man he had scarcely met.

Several months later, however, in November 1976, the names of Agee and Hosenball were inextricably linked by an announcement from the Home Secretary, Merlyn Rees. They were both

1. *Time Out*, 9.7.75.
2. *Time Out*, 20.6.75.

to be deported from Britain. There would be no proper appeal against the decision and no public discussion of the reasons. They were both said to have endangered that now familiar ogre, 'the interests of national security'.

It was certainly difficult for those shocked by this announcement to tie together these very different personalities: Agee, the ex-CIA man who had become a political campaigner for the people oppressed by his country's postwar imperialism, Hosenball, an almost apolitical figure who had developed no more than a good reporter's nose for scoops; he might appear troublesome, but hardly a threat on the same scale.

The only obvious link was the CIA itself. Both men had in different ways exposed the operations of the multinational spying organization. Both had named CIA agents. That, if anything, was the connection. And though the British government strongly denied any pressure from the Americans, the suspicion remained that the hidden hand of the Agency had been at work.

There was some substance to this theory. As far as Agee was concerned, he had never written or researched any material to do with the British intelligence services, but he was intensely disliked by the CIA. Since his book appeared, smear stories had been circulated to discredit him[1] and a clear indication given to the British authorities that his presence here was unwelcome. Two weeks before the deportation announcement, a former CIA official, James Angleton, admitted: 'We are somewhat displeased that England has given a safe haven to this person called Philip Agee.'[2]

Agee also knew well the Agency's ability to fabricate likely but false events: he had done it himself. Through a filtering process, the CIA's propaganda could well have been passed on to MI6, its British counterpart, then to MI5 and eventually to the Home Office, along the way establishing some acceptable British connection. Merlyn Rees, whose reliance on the security services

1. See page 102.
2. Quoted in the *Guardian*, 19.11.76.

had been emphasized by his recent post as Northern Ireland Secretary, need never have known its origin.

Such speculation was only encouraged by the method adopted to deport Agee and Hosenball. As American citizens they could be subjected to the powerful immigration laws, and despite their many years' residence in this country they were still described as 'visitors'. But they were not said to have broken any of the procedures laid down for their continued stay in Britain. Instead, a very specific clause in the 1971 Immigration Act relating to 'national security' was employed.

This clause had been used only once before, against an Italian, Franco Caprino (in 1974), though the suggestion that he had had contact with the IRA was never proved and the deportation order was dropped. As Liberal MP Alan Beith pointed out at the time, this inevitably led to a 'widespread belief that the order was not proceeded with because the information on which it was based was found to be false',[1] a feeling which soon surrounded the Agee–Hosenball case. Like many obscure areas of the law, it had been largely forgotten until activated by a nervous government. Even Merlyn Rees had to admit that the two Americans' cases were 'unusual'.

Two things made them particularly unusual. Firstly, the two men were never given any clear reasons as to why their deportation was, in the jargon of bureaucracy, 'conducive to the public good'. What they *were* told begged more questions than it answered. Agee was said to have 'been involved in disseminating information', to have 'aided and counselled others in obtaining information for publication' and to have 'maintained regular contacts with foreign intelligence officers'. All three activities were claimed to have been harmful to the security of the United Kingdom.

Hosenball was given a similar set of words, without elaboration. He was said, 'in consort with others', to have 'sought to obtain and obtained for publication information harmful to the security of the United Kingdom, and that this information included information prejudicial to the safety of servants of the

1. House of Commons, 6.2.75.

Crown'. It was the classic language of security, intended to alarm the general public with fears that somebody's life was at risk. But despite numerous theories thrown up during the deportation argument, the Home Office has never to this day expanded on what exactly it meant. Even Sam Silkin, the Labour Attorney-General who approved our prosecution, raised the obvious objection when this procedure was first introduced by a Tory government: 'How will the person to be deported know what is alleged against him?'[1]

The second unusual aspect was that whereas in most deportation cases there is an appeal to a tribunal, with evidence and cross-examination, the national security clause specifically excluded this. The two men would only be allowed a hearing before three advisers appointed by the Home Office itself. Again, this system had received harsh criticism from the Labour opposition, now returned to power, eliciting the comment from Roy Jenkins (later Home Secretary) that it could be used 'most dangerously and most damagingly. It is a totally unacceptable provision as it stands.'[2]

The result was that although damaging allegations had been made, they could not be satisfactorily challenged. It was almost as if the authorities had deliberately avoided the need to justify their action. As many people quickly pointed out, if Agee and Hosenball had accumulated such harmful information, why weren't they being put on trial and locked up? In fact, the case soon proved that the security apparatus was prepared to use any devious means to forestall investigation of its operations.

From the first day's press coverage, when the *Daily Express* headlined a stinging leader comment with the words 'Arrival of 1984?', it was obvious that the two Americans would not go quietly. A public campaign soon developed to get Merlyn Rees to change his mind, and the deportations became one of the most controversial decisions to be taken by the dying Labour government. At the centre of this controversy was the hastily convened Agee–Hosenball Defence Committee, of which I was a strong supporter. In the end the protest lasted over six months and was

1. House of Commons, 15.6.71.
2. In a speech, 8.3.71.

crucially diverted half-way through by the arrest of myself, Duncan Campbell and John Berry.

I was just one of many individuals and organizations angered by the deportations. There was a personal interest, of course. I knew Mark Hosenball, and had worked with him. I soon also got to know, and trust, Philip Agee. But there were some broader issues involved. Was the British government embarking on a Russian-style purge of dissident writers? Why weren't the two men being given a fair hearing? And what *were* the real reasons behind it all?

At first the Defence Committee was faced, as was its ABC successor, with an immediate problem: how to publicize an issue of no immediate emotional interest and over which the shadow of national security hung like a cloud. It struck out at the obvious target, Merlyn Rees. At a Labour Party sponsored rally in Trafalgar Square, Rees was billed as a main speaker. When it came to his turn, his words could hardly be heard above the rhythmic shouts of 'Merlyn Rees, CIA, Agee, Hosenball Must Stay'. Compared with the respectful reception given to others on the platform he can hardly have felt comfortable.

Within weeks, however, a more considered campaign emerged. Reams of press statements and background briefings were issued to explain what the argument was really about. The Home Office was the scene of regular pickets, on one occasion warranting the erection of crush-barriers. Public meetings were held up and down the country and two marches organized – one to the American Embassy, the other to Century House, the headquarters of MI6. Just before Christmas the Home Secretary was sent hundreds of special cards with a drawing by artist Patrick Proctor on the cover. Inside was a quotation from the European Convention of Human Rights: 'Everyone is entitled to a fair and public hearing within a reasonable time by an independent and impartial tribunal established by law.'

It was this aspect, that Agee and Hosenball were patently *not* getting a fair hearing, which elicited the broadest response. Leaders of twenty major trade unions, over 100 MPs, and public figures such as Jean-Paul Sartre, Jane Fonda and Spike Milligan all lent their weight to the protest. The General Secretary of the

TUC, Len Murray, was encouraged to send a personal protest to Merlyn Rees. The workers at Heathrow Airport offered more practical support: they would ground any plane on which either man was ordered to be put.

But the security authorities did not take this onslaught lying down. Depending on the gut reaction that there's no smoke without fire, they mounted their own propaganda operation. New and old smear stories about Philip Agee began to surface. He was said to have been visited by Soviet spies[1] and to be a KGB agent.[2] The Liberal leader, David Steel, was reported to have been told in confidence that Agee was responsible for the deaths of two British agents in Poland:[3] in fact Agee had never met the crucial Polish spy in this long and complicated story.

The most effective slur was connected with the murder of CIA station chief Richard Welch in Athens. Welch was killed in 1975 soon after his name had been printed in an English language newspaper, *Athens News*. Whether the motive was linked to the CIA's long-standing support for right-wing governments in Greece has never been established. But the killing had a dramatic effect.

In the United States Welch was given a hero's burial, his death used to curtail any further Congressional investigations of the CIA's activities, and Philip Agee directly blamed. The tortuous argument for this was that the man's name had also been published in an American magazine, *CounterSpy*, on which Agee had worked. But what was conveniently ignored in the controversy was that Agee had nothing to do with the naming and that *CounterSpy* had actually listed Welch as being stationed in Peru.

The origin of most of these stories can only have been the CIA. The Agency desperately wanted to discredit Agee and to discourage others from following in his wake. A crude analysis was therefore developed that if Agee had left one side he must be working for the other. In the secrecy surrounding the deportations such rumours only flourished, were readily repeated in the

1. *Daily Mail*, 18.11.76.
2. *Daily Mail*, 23.2.77.
3. *Observer*, 9.1.77.

British national press and eventually overlapped into the ABC case.[1]

At the same time, Fleet Street's uncertainty about the deportations was subtly supported by government officials. Several prominent editors were told at a Downing Street reception that the Agee–Hosenball furore had nothing to do with freedom of the press. They should play it down. The BBC even decided that no interviews with Agee should be broadcast without the prior approval of senior management. On one occasion a radio-car set up to do a live recording was actually cancelled because of this arrangement.[2]

But if most of this pressure was on Agee, who opposed it by making public statements and speeches as often as possible, Hosenball remained silent. Deeply shocked at being labelled a security risk, he fell back on the resources of his employers, the *Evening Standard*. The newspaper, then part of the powerful publishing group, Beaverbrook Newspapers, offered him money for legal costs, its potential influence in the corridors of power and publicity. In return he distanced himself from Agee, the ex-CIA man, and the noisy protesters. He retreated into a shell, hoping that the rumours that he was only the makeweight to be traded off against the real menace, Agee, would turn out to be true.

They didn't, nor did the *Evening Standard* keep up its expected campaign. The paper soon moved on to other dramas. Even a special interview between Hosenball's potentially influential father and a Home Office official proved fruitless: though they asked repeated questions, they were told nothing. As Hosenball ruefully explained later from his enforced American retreat, the intelligence services' attitude was simple: 'When the machine gets rolling, innocent people sometimes get hurt.'

The contrast between the two men's approaches was most apparent during the special hearings they were granted in January 1977. Whilst Agee held daily press conferences to reveal details of a supposedly secret process, Hosenball kept quiet. But

1. See page 155.
2. *Guardian*, 13.1.77.

the bizarre game of cat and mouse which took place at that time is worth explaining in some detail, if only because it showed the contradictions which emerge when the secrecy machine attempts to justify its actions. It proved a worthy forerunner to the ABC trial itself.

The system through which Agee and Hosenball were allowed their sole opportunity to counter the serious allegations against them was one that only the British establishment could invent. Its setting alone, the former United Service and Royal Aeronautical Club in Pall Mall, was a classic remnant from Britain's imperial past. A vast, eerily empty building of endless carpeted corridors, decorated ceilings and crystal chandeliers, it had been used most recently for a meeting of NATO military commanders, and in an upstairs room, originally set aside for lady visitors, sat the three advisers selected to listen to the case. With their bowler hats lined up outside and surrounded by paintings of famous battles, it was almost as if the two Americans had been summoned to the headmaster's study for a ticking-off.

These three advisers were in fact known generously in official circles as 'the three wise men', and their procedure was a direct copy from the secret appeals allowed to civil servants suspected of disloyalty (see page 121). This had been introduced after the case of student leader Rudi Dutschke in 1971, whose *public* hearing against deportation had thrown up embarrassing evidence of phone-tapping and letter-opening. On this occasion both press and public were carefully excluded.

For Agee and Hosenball their 'three wise men' were Sir Derek Hilton, who himself had served in British intelligence, Sir Clifford Jarrett, a former Home Office civil servant, and Sir Richard Hayward, a conservative trade union official. Their job would be to listen to what was said and then make their own independent recommendations to the Home Secretary. However, all three had in fact been hand-picked by the very same department which ordered the deportations in the first place, and if Merlyn Rees didn't like what they told him, he had every right to ignore it.

But the most extraordinary feature of these hearings was the way in which they proceeded. There was no evidence, no witness from the security services, no legal structure whatsoever. The two men were told nothing more than was in the original deportation orders. They were simply allowed to be accompanied by a friend and could introduce their own witnesses. As a result, they were effectively prosecutors at their own secret trial.

Agee went first, arriving at the Pall Mall club in the snow. For several days he described his entire life history, working from a long, carefully prepared statement. He handed in dozens of articles and interviews in which he had featured. He went through his travels, his political views, his career in the CIA. He explained that the only incidents which could possibly be construed as contact with 'foreign intelligence officers' were when he discussed publication of his book in Cuba and Russia. Every meeting he had ever had with an official of a Communist country was related to the advisers in detail, and he pointed out that he was just one of thousands of people who 'have a perfectly legitimate reason' for such discussions.

However pointless this exercise may have been, there was little else Agee could do. Even then, as he pointed out, he could well have missed some vital clue. But if he had, then the three advisers weren't telling. They sat behind their blue baize-covered table and just listened, only occasionally asking questions. You could only guess from their stony-faced expressions what they were thinking. They quickly acquired a new title – 'the silent Knights'.

When Agee had finished, a series of prominent figures gave 'evidence' on his behalf. They included journalists, MPs, American politicians and a senior official in the United Nations, Sean McBride. But what could they say, when they were proclaiming the innocence of somebody whose crimes were unknown? One former Minister, Judith Hart, was ao annoyed by the process that she marched out to confront Merlyn Rees: her mission met a predictable brick wall. The most outspoken statement came from Ramsay Clark, at one time the United States States Attorney-General. He described the hearing as 'utterly lawless'.

It gradually became obvious that the advisers themselves were uncertain of their power. Sir Derek Hilton, the chairman, admitted that he had no secret documents in front of him and no specific instructions on how to run the hearing. 'We are not altogether satisfied with what we have been told,' he said enigmatically. 'But the Home Secretary has decided this is the system. Take it or leave it.'

Agee did his best to upset the secrecy of the hearings by holding press conferences every lunchtime and evening. A battery of TV crews and rows of reporters turned up. But there was little, apart from speculation, to satisfy them. Agee revealed that he had turned on a tape-recorder at the start, and it had run until one of the advisers noticed and asked him to turn it off. Sadly, the ex-CIA agent had forgotten to press the recording button.

At the end of the hearing Agee concluded with an eloquent statement of his position. 'I do not expect the panel to share my political beliefs,' he said. 'I do expect them to understand that we will not be intimidated by accusations that we are traitors, that we are agents of foreign powers, that we subscribe to exotic and foreign ideologies, that we threaten the national security.' From their expressions there was nothing to tell whether the three advisers secretly sympathized or were, as had been suggested, merely an administrative rubber stamp.

For Hosenball there was a similarly farcical session before the 'three wise men'. He produced his own impressive series of personal referees from the world of politics and journalism, and he also described his career in great detail. After two days he genuinely believed that he had convinced the advisers of his 'innocence'. But there was no publicity and no protest.

It's unfair to suggest that nothing emerged from these hearings, and the mass of speculation, to isolate what may have angered the authorities over Agee and Hosenball. They were obviously disliked for what they represented – the new spirit of inquiry into the murky areas of security. But why had the Home Secretary been prompted into action at that particular time?

On Agee, one theory was that a visit he made to Jamaica in September 1976 could have particularly rankled. During a speaking tour of the Caribbean island he had helped the local

Council for Human Rights to identify eight CIA agents. There was some justification for this: they were said to have been using all the nastier techniques of covert action to undermine the re-election of Michael Manley's social democratic government. But Jamaica was also in the Commonwealth, and therefore firmly within the sphere of influence of the British MI6. By accident rather than design Agee could thus have trodden on more toes than just his old adversaries' in the CIA.

As far as Hosenball was concerned, there were two possibilities, either of which could have incurred the wrath of the security services. One was an article which explained how two student organizers had become involved in undercover intelligence work, particularly in Africa.[1] Hosenball was one of its authors. The other had a much more direct link with the ABC case itself. This was a two-page feature in *Time Out* entitled 'The Eavesdroppers'.

Published in May 1976, 'The Eavesdroppers' had appeared under the twin authorship of Mark Hosenball and Duncan Campbell. With a map and photographs it was the first detailed explanation of the British Signals Intelligence – radio eaves-dropping on communications – system, its links with the United States and its potential dangers and abuses. At the time it caused little interest, and there was no official reaction.

But Duncan Campbell was also one of the witnesses whom Hosenball invited to appear before the 'three wise men', and when it came to his turn he was asked specifically how the article had been researched. To their apparent surprise he said it had come entirely from public sources: phone directories, reference books, newspaper cuttings and even comments from several official spokesmen. Moreover, he explained that the vast majority of this work had been his alone. Hosenball, diverted by other more immediate news stories, had hardly been involved.

It seemed cruelly harsh if Hosenball was to be deported for an article he hadn't even written. Yet this remained the most likely candidate for the dramatic action against him. Only later, as the hammer of national security fell on the three of us, did the full significance of 'The Eavesdroppers' emerge.

1. In the *Leveller*, 2.76.

Meanwhile, both before and after our own arrest, the fierce argument about the deportations continued. Merlyn Rees announced in the House of Commons on 16 February 1977 that he had listened to what the three advisers had to say, and hadn't changed his mind. He wouldn't elaborate on what their advice might have been. The *Evening Standard* called this a 'miscarriage of justice', *The Times* 'distasteful'. Rees himself admitted that it had been, for him, 'a politically traumatic experience'.

Several attempts were made to get the courts to rule that the government's power had been misused. Agee tried to seek asylum in Scotland, where the law is technically different. He also petitioned the European Court of Human Rights. Hosenball took his case to the High Court and then to the Court of Appeal. All of these failed. Lord Denning, one of the country's most senior judges, summed up the judicial attitude. In national security cases, he said, 'our own cherished freedoms, and even the rules of natural justice, had to take second place'.[1] The government's power was, in effect, unchallengeable.

In May 1977 – over six months after the original decision – both men were finally forced to leave. Hosenball went by plane to America, Agee by boat to Europe. Their wives, and Agee's children, went with them. But Agee's belief that he was being pursued by the CIA, with the complicity of other countries, soon appeared to be confirmed.

After six weeks in France he was thrown out on the instructions of the French security service. When he tried to live in Holland he was faced with yet another deportation order. In both cases he was said to have endangered those countries' relationship with other, unspecified, nations. He has now found precarious respite in Germany; and it is some reflection of his strength of purpose that he has publicly fought all these manoeuvres – and is still writing and researching about the abuses of security.[2]

1. Court of Appeal, 29.3.77.
2. Recent harassment of Agee includes the revoking of his passport and a court order to submit any writings on his CIA experience to the Agency for clearance. Agee has also discovered that the CIA has 45,000 pages of files on him.

The deportations of Philip Agee and Mark Hosenball are important to this account for several reasons. The most obvious is that they explain the immediate background to the interview with John Berry. Without Berry's anger at their treatment he would never have decided to speak out. Without our own concern and interest, Duncan and myself would never have bothered to interview him. If the security services had intended to curtail investigation by their action, then it had exactly the opposite effect.

But the way in which the American writers were hounded out of Britain also underlined two other central issues. Firstly, that the power, and international links, of the intelligence community are such that once its tentacles expand they are almost impossible to escape. And secondly that, whatever may have happened in the United States, it remains extremely unlikely that the exposure of events such as those surrounding the Watergate scandal could happen here.

Watergate was, after all, not just about a President who tried to hide repeated attempts to cover up the scandal. Transferred to the British context, it was the equivalent of the Conservative Party deciding to snoop on the discussions of election policy at Labour Party headquarters. Its origins were also in the classic techniques of the agencies of national security: a secret break-in, bugging and surveillance. Two of the main conspirators had actually worked for the CIA. Yet the process of journalistic inquiry which led to those revelations would be virtually impossible in this country.

As far as Agee and Hosenball were concerned, the sanction against their writing was relatively clear-cut. They were foreign nationals, and could therefore be deported. But the British press itself is shackled in a number of ways which make meaningful investigation of the methods, and abuses, of the security system notoriously hard.

The contrast between Britain and America is greatest in the area of legislation. The Official Secrets Act technically prohibits all questioning of government employees about their work, outside officially recognized channels. Both sides of such an exchange, as we discovered to our own cost, are liable to prosecution. The law's provisions are so wide that they are inevitably broken every day. But its deterrent effect on the exposure of important developments, especially in the area of security, is immense.

United States law does almost precisely the opposite. Its Freedom of Information Act gives anybody the right to inspect the contents of official files or reports held by numerous government departments. Though security subjects are often excluded, this right has been regularly exercised to reveal the activities of the CIA, FBI and other agencies. One recent book on the CIA's secret drug experiments was written as a result of requests made under the Freedom of Information Act.[1]

At the same time, the sanctions against public officials who talk about their (even secret) jobs are considerably less severe in the United States. It was one of the ironies of the Agee–Hosenball case that during the course of the argument Philip Agee was informed by the United States Attorney-General that he would not be prosecuted, if he returned to America, for anything he had published in his book. Such a situation would be inconceivable in this country.

But even without this crude difference in the law, the British press is hamstrung by conventions which limit its investigative capacity. Through the parliamentary 'lobby' system, a selected group of reporters is admitted to Ministerial briefings where their confidence on certain areas is relied on. An army of over one thousand press officers employed by government departments carefully controls the flow of official information, while specialists in an area such as defence are allowed facilities and briefings only on the basis that they don't cross a closely guarded dividing-line between the public and the sensitive. 'From time to time a correspondent must ask whether the system is being used to cover up facts which in his opinion the public should know', as Andrew Wilson, former defence correspondent for *The Times*, has written.

One system in particular sums up this process of sticks – the law – and carrots – limited access to the corridors of power.

1. *The Search for the Manchurian Candidate* by John Marks (Allen Lane, 1979).

Through a series of official 'instructions' known as D-Notices, the main press and broadcasting organizations are warned that a whole range of information is considered forbidden territory. Twelve D-Notices (D for Defence) are now issued in a loose-leaf file, and cover everything from developments in new weapons and equipment to phone-tapping and the names of the heads of MI6 and MI5. They are supposed to be only advisory, but the way they work is in fact a classic example of enforced self-censorship.

Any writer or broadcaster who thinks he or she may be about to publish material included in the Notices' extremely broad categories is expected to contact the Secretary of the D-Notice Committee. The Secretary, normally a senior retired military officer, then suggests what cuts should be made. But though the Notices themselves have no legal basis, the risk of failing to comply with these requests is considerable: exclusion from the club of those entitled to the ear of officialdom and, in the background, the possibility of prosecution under the Official Secrets Act itself.

In theory, the press protects its interests by representation on the D-Notice Committee. Eleven senior executives from press and television are included among its fifteen members. But these fifteen meet only once or twice a year and all day-to-day decisions on what should or should not be published are taken by the Secretary, at present Rear-Admiral William Ash, himself a former chief coordinator of military intelligence. His immediate predecessor, Rear-Admiral Farnhill, had a similar background and one former Secretary, Colonel Lohan, explained that the system worked 'just by knowing the journalists and telling them not to do something'.

What is in practice a gentleman's agreement to protect the secret world from embarrassing disclosures has inevitably led to clashes. The most famous of these was in 1967 when *Daily Express* journalist Chapman Pincher wrote a dramatic story revealing that all overseas cables sent in or out of this country were being scrutinized by security officials. Copies of the cables were collected every day from private companies' offices, taken to the Ministry of Defence and then returned forty-eight hours later. The paper described this as a 'Big Brother intrusion into privacy'.

In fact Pincher had already consulted the D-Notice Secretary and been told that the Notices didn't apply. But the Security Service, MI 5, and the Foreign Office decided otherwise and made a last minute attempt to stop the *Express* from publishing. The paper's decision to go ahead was supported by the media as a public service and attacked by the government as a 'breach' of the D-Notice procedure.

When an official inquiry exonerated the *Express*, adding that the information was substantially correct, the government refused to accept its findings and issued its own statement. This made it clear that the D-Notice system is only as voluntary as a writer's acceptance of the official interpretation. 'Essentially,' it announced, 'the system is based on the willingness of the press to circumscribe its own freedom.'[1]

Though many writers are genuinely persuaded that the censorship is necessary in the interests of 'national security', the system has been increasingly criticized by the press and MPs. In 1980 a parliamentary committee recommended its reform, the Labour MPs voting for abolition.

During the course of the ABC case the D-Notice system made one of its most extraordinary judgements. The Secretary had been sent the manuscript of a new, updated edition of an extremely popular book, *Beneath The City Streets*.[2] This described, from publicly available sources, the network of emergency communications, including underground tunnels, which would be activated in the event of a major disaster such as a nuclear attack. But though the authorities identified twenty-eight pages which contained material considered to be damaging, they refused to say what exactly on those pages was objectionable.

The book's author, Peter Laurie, was faced with a dilemma. If he could persuade a publisher to print the book, there was the possibility of prosecution. But if he accepted the cuts, then a

1. See *The D-Notice Affair* by P. Hedley and C. Aynsley (Michael Joseph, 1967) for a full description of the Pincher case.
2. By Peter Laurie (Panther, 1979).

total of some eight thousand words – not all of which were anyway sensitive to the security services – would have to go.

It was no coincidence that this incident occurred when it did. A copy of Laurie's manuscript was among the hundreds of documents, letters and files seized from Duncan Campbell's flat the day after our arrest. Duncan, who had helped Laurie in its preparation, had been checking through the final version. For many months those papers had been sifted and analysed by the security bureaucracy, and eventually they decided to act.

In August 1977, almost three months after the more serious Section 1 charges were introduced, yet another weapon was added to the armoury against us. Duncan Campbell alone was faced with an entirely new allegation, that he had 'collected information on defence communications which might, directly or indirectly, be useful to an enemy'. This was also under Section 1 of the Official Secrets Act and therefore carried a maximum penalty of fourteen years in prison.

The basis for this new charge was precisely the information which Duncan had gathered for his journalistic work, including research for Laurie's book and the 'Eavesdroppers' article. As the prosecution later admitted, it didn't matter whether that information was publicly available or not: to them, gathering it together in one place and making deductions could still be an offence. In effect, the wheel of the deportations had come full circle. Whereas Hosenball had been expelled, his co-author, who couldn't be deported as a British citizen, was being prosecuted in the most vindictive manner. There could hardly have been a more direct attack on the type of investigative reporting the security services had grown to hate.

4

Whistleblowers

To suggest that the security authorities were mainly concerned in the ABC case to clamp down on the new spirit of investigation, and on people who simply asked awkward questions, is in fact to put only one side of the argument. Of equal concern were those who, like John Berry, had decided to speak out from the inside about their own experience. Their motive might not be that of spies, the secret furnishing of 'the enemy' with detailed information about intelligence operations, but rather to make a public statement about an organization they felt was too secret, corrupt or oppressive. But though to the security system they were still 'defectors', to anyone who could understand their motivation they were 'whistleblowers'.

The idea of whistleblowing – telling the outside world about a specific or general cause for concern within your field of work – is not new. Individuals have always felt the urge to break through the wall of silence which often hides the truth. But that feeling has been greatly encouraged by the very growth in the size of state bureaucracies, their increasing power to make decisions without external reference and the isolation of their policy-makers from any form of control. Having failed – or predicting the failure of trying – to make any headway in changing the system internally, they decide to raise the issue in a public forum.

In its broadest sense, a whistleblower can be anybody who decides that their conscience or beliefs override their loyalty to the 'company', whether a state or private employer. Not just people who work inside the agencies of national security but those from a wide range of organizations have come to that conclusion. One recent example in Britain was the civil servant Leslie Chapman who, several years afer his retirement from a senior position in the Ministry of Works (now the Property Services Agency), publicly condemned the department's secret failure to implement dramatic cost-saving programmes, such as restricting the use of chauffeur-driven cars.[1] In the United States, whistleblowers have exposed such scandals as bribery in the Chicago meat-packing industry, the award of government construction contracts to selected firms without competition, and the dangers, sometimes fatal, of a multi-million-dollar vaccination scheme.

Whistleblowers do not always make their protest in public, however. Many continue to work inside the organization, filtering out their information and suspicions to the press or watchdog bodies without ever revealing their identity. In effect they are a heightened form of a typical journalistic 'source'.

The risks involved are nonetheless great. Once suspicion has been aroused, they are liable to be downgraded or shifted to another section, if not dismissed or prosecuted. The sheer strain and isolation can by themselves be intense. Stanley Adams, for instance, who told the Common Market's anti-trust division in 1973 about secret discounts offered by the giant Swiss-based drugs company, Hoffman-La Roche, was later arrested for breaking Switzerland's 'national security' laws. Under the pressure of his expected imprisonment, his wife committed suicide.[2] There is also the danger that if whistleblowers say as much as they would really like to, their cover will effectively be blown. A document in circulation to a long list of people is one thing, a decision available to only a few another.

Although it tried, the Special Branch never succeeded, for instance, in tracking down the source of the leaked Cabinet papers which, in 1976, revealed crucial discussions within the Labour government leading to the abandonment of its much-vaunted Child Benefits scheme.[3] Nor, so far, has anyone been held responsible for similiar disclosures in *Time Out* magazine during 1979 of the Tory Cabinet's proposals to dramatically

1. See his book *Your Disobedient Servant* (Chatto and Windus, 1978).
2. Adams's experience was reported in BBC Radio 4's *Real Evidence*, 9.3.80.
3. Published in *New Society*, 17.6.76.

expand the number of nuclear power plants and to cut Social Security payments to strikers' families.[1] Cabinet documents are frequently classified 'Secret', totally covered by the Official Secrets Act, yet the issues involved in all these cases were of vital public concern. Without a whistleblower they would not have come to the surface so soon.

For those who work in the military or intelligence the opportunities to blow the whistle from the inside are far more remote. Not only do their internal structures and sanctions both discourage and in some cases prohibit such action, but the careful pigeon-holing of different areas of information makes identification of a leak that much easier. The few who have come out in public (mostly in America) have generally therefore either done so at the same time as resigning from their jobs, or waited until some time after they left.

Philip Agee was in essence a whistleblower, though he developed his disillusionment into something considerably larger than a one-off protest. But he was by no means the first and just as the investigation of the security services has been taken in the United States to an extent unheard of in Britain, so has the tradition of whistleblowing. At the same time, its political origins can be found most firmly in the watershed of recent American history – the Vietnam War.

It was precisely his experience as a Special Forces (Green Beret) officer in Vietnam which led Donald Duncan to become one of America's first public whistleblowers. In 1965, after ten years in the Army, he dramatically abandoned a promising, award-laden career, publicized his views in the radical magazine *Ramparts* and began to actively campaign against the war.

Duncan's change of mind came about principally because he started to think about the contradiction between the militant anti-communism he had been trained to espouse and the reality on the ground. United States intervention in Vietnam was based on the theory that most of the people didn't want a communist government, and yet American support for a series of corrupt Saigon regimes was only driving them further in that direction. Whilst persistent propaganda had persuaded the tax-

1. *Time Out*, 7.12.79 and 14.12.79.

paying American public that the war effort was worth its 1.5 million dollars a day, the truth was, as Duncan saw it, one of a rootless South Vietnamese army, treated like idiots by their American trainers, and whose defeat was only being forestalled by massive firepower and bombs.

Politically, Duncan was no left-winger, and retained his dislike for any form of communism. What he did see was a steadily failing strategy and, worst of all, that nobody would admit in public that this was so. 'The whole thing was a lie', he wrote soon after leaving. 'We weren't preserving freedom in South Vietnam. There was no freedom to preserve. To voice opposition to the [South Vietnamese] government meant jail or death ... I also know that we have allowed the creation of a military monster that will lie to our elected officials, and that both of them will lie to the American people.'[1]

Such views were increasingly shared by large numbers of Americans, some of whom were also veterans of the war and willing to publicize their experiences. But the mood of whistle-blowing soon spread from those directly involved in the fighting to the political decision-makers in Washington. As Donald Duncan had suggested, they were as much a part of the propaganda system as the military strategists.

The most important example of this came in 1971, when the prestigious *New York Times* newspaper began to serialize what were known as the 'Pentagon Papers'.[2] The Papers were in fact a massive 7,000-page secret report explaining and charting United States involvement in Indo-China, including Vietnam, from the end of the Second World War to 1968. They revealed for the first time not only the real extent of that involvement but how successive Presidents and their advisers had misled the American public. But though the government failed to stop their continued publication, claiming that 'the national defence interests of the United States and the nation's security will suffer immediate and irreparable harm', it did move against the man who leaked them in the first place, Daniel Ellsberg.

Ellsberg was a 40-year-old Harvard graduate who, whilst

1. *Ramparts*, 2.66.
2. Published in book form as *The Pentagon Papers* (Times Books, 1971).

working for various state departments, had shifted his views from being a hawkish supporter of the Vietnam War to active opposition. He was also one of the authors of the 'Pentagon Papers' and had access to a copy. With the help of a friend, Anthony Russo, he photocopied the document and sent it to the press.

Constructing criminal charges against Ellsberg and Russo proved more difficult than it would in this country. There is no Official Secrets Act covering all government employees with a blanket prohibition on revealing details of their work. But there *is* an Espionage Act, which covers secret codes, atomic information and 'any information relating to national defence'. Both men were eventually charged under the last heading (as well as lesser offences of theft and conspiracy), the first time that the law had been used against anybody who clearly hadn't traded secrets with a foreign power. Like Section 1 of the British Official Secrets Act used against the three of us, it was waiting to be employed by a vindictive and angry state machine.

That vindictiveness was the prosecution's downfall. During a three-month court case it was discovered that the government had both tapped Ellsberg's phone and approved a burglary at the home of his psychiatrist, part of what emerged to be a CIA-backed assessment of his 'personality'. Moreover, the two men responsible for the break-in were also involved in the developing Watergate scandal. In the end, when the prosecution failed to produce the requested results of its phone-tapping, the judge stopped the trial because of 'improper government conduct'.

In 1972 a similar attempt was made to stop publication of another whistleblower's effort, this time before he had even put pen to paper. Victor Marchetti, a CIA officer for fourteen years, had already written a fictional account of the Agency's work but now wanted to tell the real story. His interest was mainly in the covert action operations described in the last chapter, a source of growing embarrassment to the CIA, and as soon as the Agency learned of Marchetti's intention (by getting hold of a copy of his publisher's synopsis), it obtained a court injunction claiming, cleverly, that he had broken his personal contract of employment. The injunction also permitted the CIA to vet the book in advance of publication.

Only after lengthy arguments was the Agency's demand for 339 cuts (almost a fifth of the total length) reduced to 168. But Marchetti had also been encouraged by the legal action to locate another disillusioned ex-government employee, John Marks, who left the State Department over the invasion of Cambodia. Their co-authored book, *The CIA and the Cult of Intelligence*,[1] eventually proved a bestselling account of the CIA's practice and philosophy. Ironically, the fact that Marchetti was the first American author ever to be served with an official 'pre-censorship' order only added to the interest.

Since then there has been a steady stream of whistleblowers from the American secret services, most notably John Stockwell, head of the CIA's task force in Angola during 1976. Stockwell described that expensive undercover operation as 'dishonest and inefficient' and recorded his ideas and experiences in print.[2] But such individuals have also been supported by a number of organizations concerned to protect their legal rights and ability to speak out. One in particular, the Government Accountability Project, has even published a *Whistleblower's Guide to the Federal Bureaucracy*, a handbook explaining the right and wrong ways to go about it. Though still attacked by their employers, American whistleblowers now feel strong enough even to attend regular conferences where their differing experiences are described and shared.

By contrast, the pressures *not* to blow the whistle in this country are considerable, and its note of alarm has been muffled in a manner scarcely paralleled among Western democracies. To start with, there are the two million people in government employment covered by the Official Secrets Act, binding themselves to permanent silence about their work, even after they leave. They include postmen, prison officers, clerks at Social Security offices, statisticians, planners and countless civil servants. For many, the little form they have to sign may seem irrelevant, but what if one day they come across a scandal,

1. Published by Coronet, 1976.
2. *In Search of Enemies: A CIA Story* (André Deutsch, 1978).

of corruption or incompetence, which they feel demands exposure? Then those nagging doubts about the possibility of prosecution come to the surface.

Shortly after our arrest in 1977, for instance, the Act was used to punish a Social Security worker in Birmingham, John Bourn, who told the press about his poor wages. No prosecution resulted, but he was moved to a less well paid job.[1] More seriously, a man who was accidentally exposed to nerve gas while working at a government germ warfare establishment kept for many years the secret of his developing grave illness just because he was frightened of the law.[2] He was even discouraged by the Ministry of Defence from talking to his own doctor about it.

But for those employed in more 'sensitive' posts, particularly involving national security, there is a further deterrent. This is the process known as positive vetting. Affecting thousands of people in the armed forces, civil service and employed by firms working on government contracts, it is intended partly to weed out those not considered suitable for a job in the first place and partly to remind anyone who gets a post that they are being carefully watched.

Positive vetting might come into operation, for example, if a woman applied for a job as a filing clerk with the Ministry of Defence. First, she would be told to fill in a security questionnaire which asks, among other things, whether she has ever had connection or sympathies with Communists. As with the phrase familiar from the McCarthy purges in America – 'Are you or have you ever been a member of the Communist Party?' – this is a convenient label which the vetters can interpret as widely as the Special Branch interprets 'subversives'. They have done so in fact to include even supporters of Scottish Nationalism. In 1976 a lecturer at Edinburgh University was approached about the personal background of a former student subsequently employed in the Cabinet Office: the areas of interest outlined by the vetter were 'being a communist, membership of the SNP and homosexuality'.[3]

1. *Guardian*, 11.4.77.
2. Revealed on BBC TV's *Man Alive*, 29.11.77.
3. *The Times*, 19.5.76.

The Ministry of Defence would then make a check with MI5 to see whether anything was on file, a procedure known as a 'trace'. At the same time a field investigation would be set under way, carried out either by the Ministry's own security personnel (usually retired servicemen or Special Branch officers) or by MI5 itself. Friends, relatives, old schoolmates and teachers might all be followed up, as well as two specific referees. Those interviewed would be asked not just about the woman's political attitudes but also about her character and lifestyle. Does she gamble? Is she in debt? What about her sexual relationships? Her college lecturer might particularly be asked about her behaviour, mental health and politics.

Even if she got the job, she would still be re-vetted at least every five years, annually if she was under twenty-one. And if she was turned down she might never know the full reason. Her sole right of appeal – and then only if the information was to do with her political ideas as opposed to her personal life – would be to the 'three wise men' procedure used in the cases of Mark Hosenball and Philip Agee.

Like them she would be given only those details of the allegations against her which could be disclosed without 'prejudicing secret sources of intelligence'. She would hear no evidence from security witnesses. The three advisers would also have noted their official instructions to tilt the balance of their judgement, where doubts might arise, in favour of the state. In the end, she might well have been found 'guilty', as a government report into positive vetting itself pointed out, on 'no more than a question of suspicion or risk'.[1]

When this system was first introduced after the Second World War it was actually called the 'purge procedure', a clinical metaphor which smacked of thought-policing. During the 1950s the Campaign for the Limitation of Secret Police Powers claimed that 500 people had become its innocent victims. Many were refused promotion, moved to another job or dismissed, among them the assistant solicitor to ICI, John Lang, who lost his job (in which he dealt with secret government contracts) because his wife had *once* been a member of the Com-

1. *Security Procedure in the Public Services* (1962).

munist Party. The government had threatened to remove all secret work from ICI if Lang had any knowledge of it. Others were followed, questioned and probed, often on the basis of false information, wrong names, rumours and sheer paranoia. They found there was little comeback when they complained.[1]

Since then, positive vetting has been less publicized, presumably because it has been made deliberately stronger at the point of first recruitment.[2] Even a job as an instructor with the government's job training scheme was found several years ago (1975) to be covered by the 'no Communists' clause. The department agreed to withdraw this extraordinary requirement.

More recently, a man applied in 1979 for a job as a technical clerk on a Ministry of Defence contract with the electronics firm Marconi. Having filled in an eight-page form which asked for numerous personal details, including any foreign travel and the names of his grandparents, he waited for the security clearance to come through. He never heard, and only when the agency through which he'd originally applied decided to query the position were they told that the man 'was in no circumstances to be allowed on the site', and was unlikely to get *any* type of government work. No reason was forthcoming. Though unprovable, it would seem to have been the man's one-year membership of the Communist Party in the past and his involvement in student politics which gave him a black mark.

Such powerful recruiting measures apart, all civil servants are encouraged to steer clear of politics and instructed by their code of practice not to stand as parliamentary candidates. They are expected to inhabit their allotted compartment, putting loyalty to the bureaucracy first. They are told only what they need to know.

In some govenment departments secrecy becomes a job in itself, and they employ their own security teams, reporting to a number of central committees. Photocopiers are watched, offices inspected after working hours, passes checked and a note made of late workers. Pamphlets warning of the dangers of spying are

1. Cases detailed in *Reynolds News*, 31.7.60 and 7.8.60.
2. After the 1980 Blunt scandal, the procedure was in fact *tightened*, involving 33 potential stages of vetting. See the *Guardian*, 19.9.80.

issued, as well as office security manuals. Personal calls may also be sampled and monitored at the switchboard, and closed-circuit television installed. Occasionally, officers from MI5 will make their own inspection of security measures.

Documents themselves are meticulously graded into Top Secret, Secret, Confidential and Restricted – the four descending security classifications. Even the classifiers accept that 'political embarrassment' is one of the reasons for these protections. Each category also determines how the papers will be carried – in an envelope, a leather pouch or a locked box. When window-cleaners come round, sensitive papers have to be covered up, and if an official has to lock them away he could well be reminded of the security rules by a poster, such as one currently displayed, reading 'Look, Lock, Look Again. Keep Our Secrets Secret.' With Top Secret papers all copies are supposed to be individually numbered and regularly rounded up, but even above this there is a special category for 'national security' matters. The guidance for dealing with these is itself classified.

In the process of protection, dead and outdated files accumulate and many will not be released to the public or researchers for thirty years or more after they were written. Under the 'thirty year rule', established by law in 1967, they are supposed to be lodged with the Public Records Office in London for the benefit of historians. But the activities of MI6, for instance, have regularly remained outside this procedure, making its involvement at the outbreak of the Second World War unreadable until the year 2015. Before that happens, however, an official 'weeder' will have sorted through what should or should not be revealed: the Ministry of Defence alone employs thirty such 'weeders'.

The secret agencies have even tried to reclaim documents from the public domain. One report, on the surveillance of hunger marchers by the Special Branch in the 1930s, was on public file for eleven years before being suddenly removed in 1977 on the instructions of Scotland Yard. Among other things, it predicted that the marchers would use 'darts, vitriol, cudgels and firearms' when they arrived in London, none of which proved correct. It also contained a bitter attack on the personality of

1. *Guardian*, 24.8.78.

one of the leaders, Will Paynter.[1] At the time, the police justified the removal of the report by saying that it contained details
of people still alive. Equally irritating, however, must have
been its recent use by historians writing about the period; and
the report's alarmist inaccuracies, based on information supplied
by informers, inevitably raised similar concern about the
Branch's activities now.

Some of these procedures may sound time-consuming and
laughable as well as unnecessarily secretive. But if their purpose
is said to be to counter the ever-present threat of a foreign spy,
then they are equally useful against the whistleblower – the
person whose trade is not treachery but concern that the state
has gone wrong.

For John Berry, the pressures not to breathe a word about his
secret career were even greater than most. During his five years
in the Army he signed the Official Secrets Act no less than nine
times. He also went through a procedure officially called 'indoctrination'. In his particular job secrecy was a byword and
yet, seven years after leaving, he decided to speak out.

Berry was by no means the first British soldier to publicly
explain his misgivings at the task he had been given. Since the
decision to send British troops into Northern Ireland in 1969,
many servicemen have experienced the horrors of war at first
hand, not against some distant alien force but, potentially,
people to whom they might be directly related. In increasing
numbers they have returned from Ulster to talk on public
platforms and work actively against what they see as Britain's
Vietnam. Their descriptions of what life is really like for the
average 'squaddie' have added weight to the argument that the
presence of the Army on the streets of the province is both
brutalizing for the men and their targets, and no answer to a
political problem.

One officer recorded eloquently on his return that 'more
and more members of the security forces are coming to the
conclusion that they should not be in Ireland. Colonial wars
were fought in Kenya, Aden and Cyprus and many other
places. In each case their presence was disastrous. The English

Army shot Kenyans because they wanted to be Kenyans, Adenese because they wanted to be Adenese, Cypriots because they wanted to be Cypriots. Now the same army is shooting Irishmen because they want to be Irishmen.'[1]

In smaller numbers, there had also been whistleblowers from those earlier colonial conflicts. George Lennox, for instance, a Corporal who served in Aden during the 1960s, made serious allegations about Army torture of prisoners there, and claimed to have been interrogated by the Special Branch for his efforts.[2] But though John Berry had experienced none of this reality of physical warfare, he could see that the intelligence he collected was intended partly to provide the back-up for possible military intervention. He was merely removed from it by the illusory distancing of technology.

Like so many others, Berry joined the forces mainly for economic reasons. Then as much as now, 'The Professionals' attracted the jobless of the country's depressed regions by the promise of regular pay and a secure, managed environment rather than by any belief that it would be the career of a lifetime. At twenty-one, John Berry was looking for that sort of security. He had already done a number of jobs, mainly in travel agents, none of which paid very well. Ironically, he had also signed the Official Secrets Act once, while working for the National Assistance Board. But in August 1965 he was about to get married, looked forward to getting an Army house and hoped to save enough eventually to buy a place of his own.

Against the conflicting advice of his parents – 'Don't join' – and an uncle who was a Major-General – 'It will make a man of you' – he finally trod the familiar path to the local recruiting office. Encouraged by a large and jovial Sergeant, he signed on for a three-year engagement and, with his four 'O' levels, was immediately recommended for the Intelligence Corps.

At that point Berry had not much idea what this meant. It just sounded different, and more attractive than marching around on exercises. He soon discovered that the Intelligence

1. In *British Soldiers Speak Out On Ireland* (Information on Ireland, 1978).
2. *Seven Days*, 19.1.72.

Corps has two main functions within the Army's operations. One is 'counter-intelligence and security', which means protecting the physical security of regular units and guarding their secrets. The other is analysis of 'special intelligence'. In effect, this means the initial processing of the results of Signals Intelligence. John Berry opted for the second.

As already explained, Signals Intelligence (Sigint for short) is a system of listening in to other people's radio and electronic transmissions. It is used by many countries, large and small, around the world. Britain has a relatively well-developed network and the signals, invariably in code, are monitored from numerous receiving stations positioned at strategic international locations. Though the main emphasis is on military broadcasts, it is also possible to eavesdrop on diplomatic, commercial and private communications when necessary.

Once intercepted, these transmissions are then roughly analysed on site, but the results are all sent back by radio to a central decoding organization. In Britain's case this is Government Communications Headquarters (GCHQ) in Cheltenham. In turn, GCHQ passes on the most important decoded information to other organizations, notably MI6, the Ministry of Defence and its giant American equivalent, the National Security Agency.

The main advantage of Sigint over other methods of intelligence-gathering is that it is nearly always accurate. The other side can of course put out false trails, change the frequencies on which it broadcasts and switch its codes; but if successful, its reliability is considerable compared with the human agent. With technological advances, particularly in computers, it has therefore become increasingly employed in postwar spying. But its very growth, its potential for international political manipulation and its use against non-military targets have also made Sigint more and more controversial, as we shall see in the next chapter.

Corporal Berry was never more than a small cog in this enormous multinational machine. But it was soon made clear to him that what he was involved in was 'sensitive' work. At his very first briefing session he was put through the process of 'indoctrination', the coldly sinister official terminology – a lecture intended to encourage his future silence with the threat of the Official Secrets Act.

Yet it was also more than that. Indoctrination ushered him into membership of a secret elite. He was being made party to knowledge which most people couldn't be trusted with. It was rather like the Freemasons, with its special mumbo-jumbo, private names and codes and its own secret camaraderie. To those outside the club he could say nothing; to those inside he could speak only if they had been indoctrinated to the same level of secrecy. Right from the start his special position was emphasized by physical segregation.

There was also a parallel process to indoctrination called 'de-indoctrination'. This did not, as it suggests, allow him to talk more freely, but rather the opposite. Whenever he moved outside his regular unit, or to a different country, he was told, through the de-indoctrination procedure, that he could not discuss his work even within the closed group of club members. He switched off, only to be switched on again when he returned to base. Throughout his four years in Sigint this ritual was a constant reminder of the rules of the game, rules he wasn't expected to question. 'It was constantly rammed down one's throat the extent to which you were liable to very serious penalties if you disclosed anything at all,' as he told us during the interview.

Berry was also, of course, positively vetted by the system of personal and political checks already described. The extent of this operation was suggested by a then unexplained hold-up in his being approved. On reflection, his only conclusion was that it was to do with a school-friend's father, who happened to be in the Communist Party.

Eventually, after a three-month training course with a Signals squadron near Loughborough, Berry was posted to a monitoring base on the Mediterranean island of Cyprus. There, for almost three years, he worked in the front line of Signals Intelligence – no guns or tanks, just a steady stream of radio messages waiting to be analysed. As at most Sigint bases, a team of radio operators would listen in to networks of radio signals and either write down or record what they heard. The raw results would then be passed on to analysts, whilst other staff would use direction-finding equipment to locate the positions of the communicating parties. But the most complicated analysis and decoding was done at GCHQ in Cheltenham. Berry didn't know what happened to the results, and wasn't encouraged to ask.

As soon as he arrived, he was given yet another security lecture and was not allowed into a special compound, known as 'the block', until his processing was complete. A sign outside this compound read, 'What you see here, what you do here, what you hear here, when you leave here, let it stay here.' He passed it every day as he went to work, checked through a turnstile.

Secrecy even covered naming of the base itself, part of Britain's large, residual land-holding on an island it once controlled. At the entrance it was publicly labelled 9th Signals Regiment – no mention that personnel from the Intelligence Corps worked there or that it had anything to do with intelligence-gathering. This was intended to crudely mask its real function as a listening, as opposed to an ordinary communications, post.

Berry quickly discovered that this subterfuge, at least, didn't work, and appeared to have more to do with maintaining the internal regime that secrecy on everything was paramount. Many people on the island knew more or less what 9th Signals Regiment was doing. Its tall array of receiving aerials could be seen up to ten miles away. Some Cypriots even came to work right inside the security compound – doing general maintenance work on the building – and would be able to hear the supposedly secret bleepings of monitoring equipment.

But for over a year John Berry was perfectly happy with his job in Cyprus. Though sometimes boring, it was a secure, reasonably comfortable life in a particularly beautiful spot. He scarcely stopped to think about it. Only gradually did he begin to ask some fundamental questions.

In his spare time he started to read books, not only about politics but also the history of Cyprus, and its repeated colonization through the centuries. The island had been independent since 1960 and yet Britain still maintained several military stations, including 9th Signals Regiment, within what was

The snoopers snapped. Members of the Special Branch team who arrested Aubrey, Berry and Campbell

Chief Superintendent Harry Nicholls – Photo: *Time Out* Picture Library

Chief Inspector Moffat – Photo: Andrew Wiard (Report)

Sergeant Shaw – Photo: *Time Out* Picture Library

Inspector Battye

The watchers and listeners

top left Police helicopter with ball-shaped mounting containing film or video camera with telephoto lens powerful enough to pick out faces in a crowd – Photo: Andrew Wiard (Report)

left Surveillance of the Notting Hill Carnival from Westway flyover. The video camera has a light intensifier in front for use at night – Photo Andrew Wiard (Report)

above Telephone-tapping equipment

Some of the leading personalities

After the end of their trial: Aubrey (left), Berry (right) and Campbell (centre), who holds part of the prosecution case against him, his photo of the London Post Office Tower – Photo: Andrew Wiard (Report)

Philip Agee – Photo: Andrew Wiard (Report)

Merlyn Rees, Home Secretary – Photo: Press Association Photos

Mark Hosenball – Photo: Angela
Phillips

Sam Silkin, Attorney-General –
Photo: Mike Wells

London's secret landmarks

93 Ebury Bridge Road, the phone-tapping centre. The inset shows a close-up of the sign outside – Photo: Chris Schwarz

Curzon Street House, the headquarters of MI5 – Photo: Chris Schwarz

Euston Tower with its white-curtained sixteenth floor indicating the MI5 offices. – Photo: Chris Schwarz

Century House, the headquarters of MI6 – Photo: Chris Schwarz

overleaf The London Post Office Tower, showing microwave receivers and transmitters – Photo: Andrew Wiard (Report)

known as the Sovereign Base Area. To all intents and purposes this 100-odd square miles was, and still is British territory, with street-names like Isle of Wight Avenue and Winchester Terrace. How could this continuing imperialism be justified, he asked.

In fact, as we discovered when we prepared our defence against the ABC prosecution, the British bases on Cyprus had been the subject of much political controversy. Opposition parties had regularly demanded their closure, they were viewed as unnecessary intrusions of superpower politics, and during a visit to the island in 1978 by Denis MacShane, then President of the National Union of Jounalists, he was met with incredulity when he explained that a conversation about them was the subject of an Official Secrets trial. 'We have published photographs of all these installations,' one daily newspaper editor told Mac-Shane. 'Everyone knows what goes on inside them.'[1] During the trial itself, the delicate *political* status of the bases – as opposed to their day-to-day function – was also brought up to stop public identification of 9th Signals Regiment's real purpose (see page 177).

There was also the question of what use was made of the information collected through eavesdropping. Berry knew that the British network was closely allied to that of the United States, and the Vietnam War was then at its height. To what extent was Britain, either tacitly or openly, supporting such aggressive interventions through its Sigint operations? He could see that Cyprus was strategically useful for listening to the Middle East. But wasn't its purpose more to do with supporting repressive regimes like that in Iran, with the economic importance of its oil, than any military strategy against the Soviets?

All this made Berry think more about the pervasive secrecy. The effect of it had been to dehumanize him, to turn him into an unthinking machine. But once you began to question it, then the machine broke down. From absurd examples, like the identity of the unit where he worked, he moved outwards to query the whole system and whether it wasn't there less to protect against Russian spies than to keep the British public in

1. *New Statesman*, 30.6.78.

the dark. (During the course of the ABC case another ex-Sigint worker, Bill Hetherington, wrote in *Peace News* that during his indoctrination 'it was pointed out that the reason for secrecy was not to prevent the Russians, or indeed any foreign power, from knowing of our activities, as they would clearly be aware of them from their own intelligence sources; it was to prevent the ordinary public from knowing what we were doing – that was the supreme danger.')[1]

Such doubts didn't come together into a clear political analysis, nor were they ever voiced openly. Only with a few close friends did he ever feel able to discuss the rights and wrongs of what they were doing. But this was enough to make him think seriously about getting out. Unfortunately, he had already extended his contract to a full nine years' engagement, a decision encouraged by the higher pay he would receive. He inquired about 'discharge by purchase' – buying himself out – and was told this was at the discretion of the Army, a privilege they weren't prepared to grant. It was not going to be easy.

By chance, one particular incident brought Berry's decision to a head. At a drunken party in Famagusta one evening, he and some friends decided to phone up the Sergeants' Mess at 9th Signals Regiment, where an annual dance was then in progress. They pretended that a bomb had been planted in the building, and though they never thought it would be taken seriously, it was. The dance was abandoned while an eventually fruitless search took place. A further search then ensued to find the culprits.

When Berry and his two friends were unmasked – without very much difficulty because a security officer was present at the party – they were immediately suspended from work in the security compound. They were all court-martialled and Berry was reduced to the rank of Lance-Corporal. Four months later he was posted back to England and given the choice of transfer to another Corps or discharge. He happily opted for the latter, receiving a testimonial that 'he should do well at whatever he turns his hand to'.

Once out of the Army, Berry soon settled in to a completely

1. *Peace News*, 25.8.78.

new civilian life. He started training to become a social worker. It seemed far more useful employment than his clandestine work in Sigint, and it wasn't until six years after his discharge that he was brought back to the subject of secret listening with a jolt.

Flipping through a copy of *Time Out* magazine one day, he came across the 'Eavesdroppers' article. He was amazed at how much information it contained about Signals Intelligence, even mentioning his own unit in Cyprus. If these two writers had found out so much just by diligent research, then it put the lie to much of what he had been told during his brief career.

His head began to buzz again with ideas. As a social worker he had seen the effects of the government's cuts in expenditure on all kinds of welfare schemes – hospitals, schools, education. And yet Sigint was so protected that its budget wasn't even publicly known, let alone considered for pruning. There was definitely something wrong.

When he read about the proposed deportations of Philip Agee and Mark Hosenball, his thoughts coalesced. Here was national security being used to expel two people from Britain without any clear reason at all. It was directly linked to his own previous job through Hosenball's connection with 'The Eavesdroppers', whilst Agee was a person from inside the system who had changed his mind – someone with whom Berry could directly identify. He decided it was the right time to do something similar.

John Berry thought long and hard about whether or not he should make a public statement. He was well aware of the risks involved, though the forms he had signed only mentioned Section 2 of the Official Secrets Act, not Section 1. But against that he could set a number of arguments. One was that when he left the Army he had agreed not to travel to any Communist country for two years. The reason for this was made clear: after that he wouldn't have any information still relevant to an enemy. At the same time he didn't have very much to add, in terms of detail, to what had appeared in 'The Eavesdroppers'. As a Corporal, he just didn't know.

What he did have were the opinions of someone who had

worked in this secretive area. Maybe his lead would encourage others to come forward and start a process of public debate on the intelligence service, as had happened in the United States over the CIA. That was his hope, the expectation of many whistleblowers that their isolated example will set a ball rolling. But before very long his worst fears were realized.

5

The Anonymous Colonel B

It might seem that we have come a long way from the Special
Branch tapping a phone in London to the international eavesdropping in which John Berry was involved. But the distance is
all too easily bridged. In the United States the giant National
Security Agency (NSA), officially concerned with overseas
monitoring, had been discovered intercepting the communications of thousands of private citizens, especially those involved
in protest movements. For many years, the entire daily output of
three large cable companies was collected by the NSA, checked
through for specific names and the results passed on to the
American equivalents of MI6, MI5 and the Special Branch.
Until the possible illegality of this operation was pointed out in
the early 1970s, over 150,000 messages were read and analysed
each month. Among the targets were actress Jane Fonda and
author Benjamin Spock.[1]

In Britain, a mixture of secrecy, security and tradition have
combined to mask any such disclosures. Those who work in
Signals Intelligence are told that the need for secrecy 'never
expires' – unless they do first. And ironically, it wasn't until the
ABC case, which was intended to maintain the deadly silence,
that any official recognition was granted to the postwar development of this expanding area of intelligence-gathering.

Intercepting other people's secret messages, and breaking the
codes in which they are written, is at least as old as the Ancient
Egyptians.[2] But whereas it was then a matter of sitting down
with a piece of paper and working through the possible combi-
nations, it is now a far more sophisticated operation. Just as
radio technology has increased the potential of international

1. *Washington Post*, 13.10.75.
2. For a history of code-breaking, especially in the Second World War, see
The Codebreakers by David Kahn (Sphere, 1973).

communications, filling the atmosphere with signals and bouncing them back and forth from satellites, so the codes themselves have become so complex that in some cases they are virtually uncrackable.

Modern Signals Intelligence not only encompasses Comint (communications intelligence), John Berry's area of work, but Elint (electronic intelligence) and Radint (radar intelligence). Sounds, patterns and the extent of signals traffic can sometimes yield information as useful as the messages themselves. The monitoring equipment itself is so sensitive that from a single array of aerials measuring 500 yards in diameter,[1] it is possible to listen in simultaneously on hundreds of signals coming from any direction, including short-range radio messages transmitted thousands of miles away. Processing the results has created an expensive game of chess in which computers battle to discover the vital key to an opponent's code.[2]

At the hub of the British Sigint network is Government Communications Headquarters (GCHQ) in Cheltenham. Inside two large office blocks at either end of the Gloucestershire country town, hundreds of people sit in special cubicles – listening, decoding, translating and analysing. At their service is a giant American computer, and both sites are surrounded by tall barbed-wire fences. Around the world, an estimated 20,000 people work for GCHQ, whether directly or indirectly and its cost, though never disclosed, is thought to be over £200 million a year. These figures make it by far the largest and most expensive of the British spying organizations.

Reading the recruiting advertisements for GCHQ, you would think it had something to do with 'research' into communications. Those who apply are left in little doubt that it is primarily concerned with intelligence. Even before they join, new recruits have to sign the Official Secrets Act during briefing sessions and are asked to account for every year of their lives. One woman applicant who mentioned that she was going to Russia for a holiday was advised firmly against. With the tedious

1. An aerial like this is sited at Chicksands, Bedfordshire.
2. Useful articles on Sigint can be found in the American magazines *Ramparts* (8.72) and *Penthouse* (11.75), and the *New Statesman* (2.2.79).

routine and a social life deliberately limited to those in the same job, she also decided against the secret career.

In fact GCHQ's own decorative crest gives its game away, showing signals flashing busily backwards and forwards across a globe. Apart from Cyprus, where John Berry was stationed, the Cheltenham complex coordinates the efforts of listening stations in Germany, the Far East, Africa, Australia and the Middle East, as well as this country – up to twenty in all. They are manned round the clock both by members of the civilian Composite Signals Organization and by personnel from all three armed services, and linked by relay stations to GCHQ. A rare mention of these overseas listening bases in the British national press was a *Daily Mirror* report in 1979 that a woman had complained to an industrial tribunal about GCHQ's refusal to post her to the all-male base on the South Atlantic island of Ascension. Aircraft and naval vessels also join in the regular eavesdropping.

One reason why GCHQ maintains this extensive network is a long-standing agreement with four other countries – the United States, Canada, New Zealand and Australia. Together, they effectively monitor the world, dividing it up into areas of responsibility and sharing some, though not all, of the results. This international pact, first signed as long ago as 1947, is itself considered so secret that its existence became an issue during the ABC trial.

The major partner in this treaty is the American National Security Agency. Controlled from a well-protected windowless headquarters building at Fort George Meade in the Maryland countryside, the NSA commands over 100,000 employees and literally hundreds of listening posts, ships and planes (four of its sites being in Britain), and costs even more to run than the CIA. Its intelligence is allegedly so effective that it can prejudge the plans of foreign governments, determine precisely what their armed forces are doing, 'fingerprint' the voices of individual radio operators and can even disentangle the split-second 'squirts' of information shot from nuclear submarines to orbiting satellites.

In turn, the British system depends on the NSA for much of

its information, particularly through satellite reconnaissance, and though technically controlled by the Foreign Office, it is basically subservient to its transatlantic big brother. During a civil servants' strike in 1979 (affecting GCHQ) their union agreed to continue servicing 'the American link' in the interests of 'national security'.[1] And though the NSA has received more public attention, it is still as fundamentally secretive. One version of its initials runs: 'Never Say Anything'.

Despite the size and secrecy of this operation, it is all too easy to see Signals Intelligence as neutral, involving no risk to human life, no provocation. Instead of sending out a human spy, all you need to do is monitor from a safe distance and interpret the results. As with all developments in technology, this remains a myth. The computers which whir round ceaselessly at GCHQ are no more or less important than the human agents who control them, and the very expansion of Sigint in the past twenty years into a giant, multinational exercise in itself raises questions about how that control is exercised.

American defence chiefs prefer to emphasize the importance of Sigint, and other technical spying methods, in finding out where, when and how the Soviet Union is testing and developing new nuclear weapons. They argue that this is vital to the East–West balance of power. At our trial, British Sigint was described as a vital component in the 'defence' of any country using it. But that is clearly only part of the story. Sigint provides essential back-up to the aggressive interventions of Western powers in world affairs, especially those of the United States. Its justification is specifically phrased in terms of a crude anti-communism, whether the threat is real or not.

Deliberate provocation has in fact become a regular feature of Sigint work itself. Ships and aircraft have been sent into foreign sea- and airspace, often with the frightening intention of triggering the other side's defence communications into action, thus giving the distant monitors a truer picture. In some cases ships have been attacked, submarines have collided and planes have been shot down in this deadly game of cat and mouse. Examples of this include an Israeli attack on the

1. *Guardian*, 14.3.79.

spy-ship USS Liberty in 1967 and collisions between Soviet and American submarines off the Russian coast, reported in 1975.

Sigint is also not just about military information. Political and economic information – from embassies, private companies and other sources – is all sucked in by the sweeping monitors. For instance, from one of its British sites, Menwith Hill in Yorkshire, the NSA is said to listen in on thousands of international calls – looking for political and business information.[1] Ever since the 1967 revelation that overseas cables were being scrutinized by British security officials (see page 111), it has been assumed that GCHQ indulges in similar interception. During negotiations for membership of the Common Market, Cheltenham was reported to be busy deciphering the negotiating stances of our prospective European partners. Such examples place Sigint firmly at the centre of political controversy and also raise the question of its illegality under international diplomatic law.

Even the siting of Sigint listening stations can involve major political issues. The NSA has spent millions of dollars on secret military and economic aid to countries in order to ensure the continuance of monitoring facilities – sometimes without the knowledge of United States politicians. When the United States withdrew its pressure on the Turkish government to halt the illicit export of heroin, for example, this did not reflect a sudden change in its attitudes to drug trafficking. It was directly related to the treasured existence of a chain of NSA bases along the Turkish border with Russia.

But the secrecy surrounding Sigint has also hidden its technical weakness. The NSA now collects so much information, a lot of it useless, that it simply cannot process the results fast enough. At Fort Meade a 'classified waste destructor' can handle up to twenty tons of paper every day, the excreta of an unstoppable colossus. The military codes of the major powers are also said to have become so hard to break that Sigint has inevitably shifted its emphasis to easier targets – third world governments, economic intelligence and internal 'subversives'. As one leading American Congressman, Senator Frank Church, has commented,

1. *New Statesman*, 18.7.80.

this technology could at any time 'be turned around on the American people ... the capacity is there to make tyranny total.'

The power of the Sigint agencies to fend off any further investigation of its practice and uses has, however, proved enormous. When, during the mid-1970s, the Australian Prime Minister Gough Whitlam began to question the role of secret American bases in his country, he found himself at the receiving end of heavy covert pressure. Whitlam suspected that a supposed 'defence and research' centre at Pine Gap near Alice Springs (secretly run by the CIA) might in fact be used by the Americans to gather information on Australian companies, as well as political activists. (Some time later it was revealed that Pine Gap *was* involved in such activity, as well as electronic spying, and that 7,000 Australians were on file at the United States National Agency's European headquarters in Frankfurt.) But before Whitlam could air the subject fully in public, he was dismissed dramatically by the Governor-General, Sir John Kerr, in November 1975 – for the reason that he had lost parliamentary support. The day before, the CIA had warned its Australian counterpart in a secret telegram that unless 'this problem' could be solved, it would withdraw cooperation on security.[1]

In Scandinavia, a series of 'secrets' trials have all involved investigations into Sigint. During 1969, a Danish reporter was convicted and fined for disclosing the existence of a network of listening posts in his country. In 1973 two Swedish journalists and a former secret service agent were all gaoled after magazine articles had exposed embarrassing details of 'neutral' Sweden's apparent co-option into both American and British monitoring and surveillance activities. Most recently, two Norwegian writers and their source were found guilty in 1979 of 'damaging the national security': information they had gathered covered not only monitoring bases in Norway but lists of Special Branch officers obtained by simply making phone calls. Their trial

1. See *The CIA's Australian Connection* by Denis Freney (Denis Freney, 1977).

bore marked similarities to our own, with parallel overkill by the prosecution.

As already suggested, such inquiries have not left GCHQ totally unscathed. British Sigint has been linked to provocative incidents, the monitoring of allies as well as intercepting communications within the United Kingdom. It was a team from GCHQ in Cheltenham which was said to be responsible for preparing a bug planted inside 10 Downing Street during Harold Wilson's premiership (see page 43). But whilst the American NSA has at least been subjected to some public examination, its smaller partner has fought long and hard to avoid any similar exposure.

The most recent example of this came in 1980, when a series of allegations by a former GCHQ officer, Jock Kane, were published in the *New Statesman*.[1] Kane, a loyal veteran of thirty-two years' Sigint experience, claimed that corruption was rife within the organization and security procedures lax. At the Hong Kong base where he worked – mainly targeted at Communist China – dozens of secret documents had gone missing over a number of years, almost certainly into the hands of enemy agents. Of equal concern was that GCHQ officers in Hong Kong had indulged in a number of expenses fiddles, one involving a company actually run by a former senior officer at the base, Frank Wilks. Apart from the dangers of blackmail such activities entailed, their very existence had been encouraged by what Wilks himself described as the 'freelance' nature of GCHQ's budget. 'They can spend what they like,' he said in an unguarded moment.

But though Kane had tried hard within the organization to have the system improved, he had been persistently fobbed off or threatened with the Official Secrets Act. To hide the missing documents, for instance, the records were simply doctored, whilst two official inquiries into the corruption allegations had petered out though lack of cooperation from GCHQ. When my co-defendant Duncan Campbell, now working for the *New Statesman*, and a *Daily Mirror* reporter followed up Kane's

1. *New Statesman*, 16.5.80 and 23.5.80.

story, they found themselves the subject of phone-tapping. surveillance and an elaborate GCHQ plan to stop anyone talking. An ITV programme on the subject was also stopped by a nervous Independent Broadcasting Authority, arguing the threat to 'national security',[1] and the government itself said that deficiencies had been 'corrected'. In fact, the newspapers' investigations resulted in a former accommodation officer at the Hong Kong base being charged with corruption in the colony.

As Kane himself commented: 'The Official Secrets Act is not used against those who cause genuine breaches of security. It is used as a deterrent against those whose words might set in motion criticism of the privileges, inefficiency and arbitrary power of the secret security bureaucracy.' What was significant was not so much the seriousness of his allegations but the determination of GCHQ to cover them up. The double standard of these continuing internal scandals compared with our own treatment was clearly underlined.

But even before the ABC case there were tell-tale signs that no public discussion of GCHQ's expanding empire would be tolerated. In 1958, two Oxford undergraduates wrote a brief description in their university magazine, *Isis*, about the dangers of provocative missions by small boats inside Russian territorial waters. They knew this from first-hand experience of Sigint during National Service, and both were prosecuted under the Official Secrets Act, receiving nominal sentences.

Fifteen years later, a former British diplomat and one-time Foreign Office adviser to MI6, Geoffrey McDermott, was about to publish a book entitled *The New Diplomacy*. Mostly about changing patterns in international relations, it contained just one paragraph about the work of GCHQ, explaining no more than that the organization intercepted and decoded messages. Even that was too much for the advisers to the D-Notice Committee, to whom the book was sent. The paragraph

1. After cuts, the programme was eventually broadcast as a *World in Action* report (9.6.80). In it, David Ennals, a Foreign Office Minister at the time of Kane's original allegations, said he hadn't realized how serious they were and called for a 'high-level inquiry'. No such inquiry has so far taken place.

was rewritten, and when McDermott was scheduled to appear on a TV documentary posing outside the main gates of Cheltenham, that sequence, lasting just over a minute, was also cut by the Independent Broadcasting Authority. Most extraordinary of all in this bizarre episode was that McDermott had politely described the work of GCHQ as 'well worth maintaining'.

But it was a rare whistleblower from inside Sigint, American as opposed to British, who provided the impetus for the 'Eavesdroppers' article in *Time Out*, the most detailed description to have appeared at that time about GCHQ. Winslow Peck was a former analyst with the NSA, a highly successful careerist who turned sour after a year's stint in Vietnam. By that time he knew a great deal about the NSA's operation and could point to both its dangers and its links with GCHQ. During early 1976 he visited London and talked to Mark Hosenball and Duncan Campbell, though he knew little about the detailed working of British Sigint. In one of several interviews he gave to journalists during that visit, he even pointed out the problems of exposing similar facts about GCHQ. 'You have laws – the Official Secrets Act,' he said, 'which would prevent us doing our work.'[1]

Yet with the publication of 'The Eavesdroppers' in May 1976, it appeared that the blanket suppression of all reference to GCHQ had stopped. True, *Time Out* was not a national publication and it didn't have the authority of a TV programme, but there was no official protest. What nobody realized clearly at the time was that behind the scenes the storm clouds were gathering. For the article had indeed caused a fuss in the secret corridors of power.

With the benefit of hindsight it is possible to trace the progression of the reaction. In July 1976, when Winslow Peck attempted to return to Britain, he was refused entry at Heathrow Airport on the unexplained but legal grounds that his exclusion was 'conducive to the public good'. Four months later, Mark Hosenball was served with a deportation order. At the same time, Duncan Campbell became a marked man,

1. *Street Life*, 17.4.76.

and when John Berry decided to talk about his direct experience of Sigint, the scene was set for a confrontation between the secret world and those who queried its function.

What did John Berry actually have to say about Signals Intelligence during that three-hour interview? For some of the time he talked about his personal history – how he had joined up, the pressures and secrecy once he was inside and how his disillusionment had eventually been galvanized by the Agee–Hosenball case. Much of this I have already described, and bore noticeable similarities to the experience of his American counterpart, Winslow Peck. He then went on to describe what he knew about how his part of British Sigint worked – its estimated size, its structure and where some of the units were located. He said his own main task had been to chart the activities of the Iraqi army, a particularly tedious job. He also mentioned a few, very general, examples of how Sigint had succeeded, for instance in monitoring the planned sailing of the Turkish fleet towards Cyprus and the panic when the Israeli air force struck unexpectedly at the Egyptians in June 1967. The latter case was hardly a great coup since the Egyptians had, in their confusion, abandoned all attempts at code.

Occasionally, more mysterious aspects of Sigint would enter the conversation, usually prompted by Duncan's notes for 'The Eavesdroppers', some of which he had brought along. There was reference to a central collection of Sigint intercepts, located somewhere in Britain. We were also surprised to learn that information from the hated Iranian secret police, Savak, apparently found its way from the Americans into the British Sigint network. A lot of this, for a comparative innocent in the area, was well above my head, but at the end Duncan told me that he had in fact added virtually nothing to what he already knew.

What we were in fact listening to were the ill-recollected memories of someone who, seven years before, had played a small part in the eavesdropping network. If an article had appeared in *Time Out* as a result of the interview, it would have centred on Berry's own attitudes and concern as an insider, not on the few factual details he could muster. But to the secret world, the very fact that John Berry had attempted to prod his memory into action, whether accurately or not, was something which could not be permitted.

The power of GCHQ and its satellite monitoring organizations cannot therefore be easily exaggerated. At the time of our arrest the man in charge of advising the Prime Minister about security and intelligence was Sir Leonard Hooper. For over thirty years before that appointment, Hooper had worked at Cheltenham, latterly as its director. But when the decision was taken to prosecute the three of us for our tape-recorded conversations it was not Sir Leonard who was given the task of publicly defending the eavesdroppers. That privilege went to a man who had no name at all – the anonymous Colonel B.

If anyone came to personify the secret world which formed the background to our prosecution, it was Colonel B. It wasn't just his ridiculous anonymity, though that in itself eventually brought more attention to our case than it had ever received before. It was his whole way of thinking, a philosophy in which the secret stamp, the security check and the process of indoctrination were the fundamental precepts. Those who escaped from that, as John Berry had, must either deny its existence or be labelled subversive.

The Colonel himself was a classic career officer. A product of Sandhurst, the elite Army training college, he had been a soldier all his adult life. He had joined up in 1949 at the age of eighteen, straight out of school. Since then he had passed through several military academies and was well imbued with the Army ideology.

His experience of Signals Intelligence was comparatively recent, however. Five years before he emerged into the limelight, he had been transferred to take command of 9th Signals Regiment in Cyprus, the very same unit where Berry had served. This was largely an administrative job and he had not seen a lot of the day-to-day grind. But with his Sandhurst training he was soon moving up the hierarchy. He became the overall head of British Army Sigint, part of the intelligence staff at the Ministry of Defence in London.

After a subsequent visit to one of the units under his command, the Colonel had achieved a rare piece of publicity. He had been described humorously in an Army magazine as 'the Godfather of our sponsored precinct in the communications underworld'. It was a veiled reference to the then popular Mafia film starring Marlon Brando, and to the undercover work of Signals Intelligence, 'sponsored' by GCHQ. But if in reality the Colonel was hardly that sinister, he was also unlikely to have been amused. You could scarcely see him sharing a pint and a joke in the officers' mess. He was far more likely to be sitting at his desk deciding into which security category he should place a particular document.

As far as the Colonel was concerned, any public reference to Sigint was damaging. Ever since he himself had been indoctrinated it had never entered his head to talk about Sigint to anyone outside the closed world of the intelligence community. The entire subject was classified at the highest level, and classified matters could only be discussed with someone who had the same security clearance. That didn't include journalists.

He had always studiously avoided any contact with the press. He considered even his personal views, especially on politics, to be a private matter and not to be divulged to outsiders. As he later explained, he had only once had the opportunity to talk to reporters during his secret career. This was at the time of the Turkish invasion of Cyprus when he bumped into a television crew by chance. He could remember courteously declining their request for an interview.

But though the Colonel had been trained to believe that the general public should remain totally ignorant of what he was doing, within the organization itself he also operated on another important principle. This was the 'need to know'. Every aspect of the work was tightly compartmentalized so that those in any specific area knew only so much and no more. To step outside that specialization was to immediately endanger the security of the system, to lay an individual open to potentially damaging interrogation by the 'enemy'.

It was therefore not surprising that the Colonel was simply unaware of many of the broader aspects of his work. He didn't know about some of the latest developments in technological spying, such as satellite photography. He certainly hadn't read about the activities of the NSA in America, or the in-investigations of its 'crimes'. He had no idea that a considerable amount had been published in the United States about the operations of Signals Intelligence. If he didn't need to know, he had been told, he just didn't know.

With this limited vision, his attitude towards 'The Eaves-droppers' article was almost inevitable. When he was shown it by his superiors at the Ministry of Defence he could only agree that it contained material 'damaging to the national interest'. It should never have been written. He wasn't told what happened as a result – that was not his responsibility – but many months later he was in for a further surprise.

The Colonel was handed a copy of our tape-recorded conversation. Reading through its 200-odd pages, all marked Top Secret, he could only conclude that this was an even greater danger to the nation. Along with a dozen other officials at the Ministry he gave his opinion: the damage to Sigint, in their combined assessment, ranged from 'harmful' to 'extremely grave'.

It was roughly half-way through the lengthy progression of the ABC case towards our eventual trial that Colonel B was given the opportunity to air his views in public. By that stage – November 1977 – almost nine months had passed since the interview with John Berry and our sudden arrest by the Special Branch. The wheels of justice had moved ponderously and there had been delays whilst either the prosecution considered its next move or the defence requested more time to study the growing list of charges and evidence.

With the addition of the separate allegation against Duncan Campbell that he had 'collected information on defence communications', we now faced a total of seven charges under the Official Secrets Act, most of those within the punitive Section 1. The evidence against us covered hundreds of pages of photocopied documents and statements, all bound into volumes as thick as telephone directories. Meanwhile, as we made regular visits to our respective legal advisers, we were also forced to continue the daily pilgrimage to our local police stations, signing in a book the proof that we hadn't disappeared overnight. This tedious process could take several hours out of each week and disrupted our social life.

Predictions about the outcome of the case also continued to be gloomy. There was a growing conviction that John Berry, at least, would go to prison for a number of years. The only good sign was that so many people were supporting the protest at our prosecution, spearheaded by the ABC Campaign. But though there had been regular demonstrations and publicity every time we appeared in court (usually to hear about some further delay) and a great deal of curiosity about what we might have done, there had so far been not one jot of publicly revealed explanation to support our treatment as spies.

The first opportunity for this would be the committal hearing, a necessary formality to pass any prosecution on from the magistrates to a higher court. Having listened to the evidence, the justices would then decide whether there was a case to answer. And if there was one factor which weighed particularly heavily against us, it was that the main witness for the prosecution would be completely nameless.

Anonymous witnesses are unusual in court cases. Letters of the alphabet normally replace a person's real name only where blackmail is involved, or where there is a genuine threat of personal danger, or on the rare occasion of a spying trial. If the prosecution felt we came nearest to the last category, then they should not have been surprised when we objected. But as soon as the issue was raised at the committal proceedings there was a fierce argument.

The first choice as the man from Sigint whose evidence would send us on the road to the Old Bailey was not, however, Colonel B at all. It was another officer, who was to be named merely as Lieutenant-Colonel A. The justification for this was simple: the danger to national security if he was identified in public. 'There are times,' intoned the prosecutor Michael Coombe, 'when ordinary rules cannot be followed and the court has to weigh individual justice against the interests of the community.' It seemed clear, nonetheless, that the community being protected was that of the intelligence world, and not the wider public.

Through our barristers we protested strongly at this procedure. They argued that anonymity was being used to give an unfair atmosphere of sinister danger to the hearing. After all, even explosives experts in Irish bombing trials gave their names. The next step would be for no live witnesses at all, only voices from behind a curtain, as had happened in Northern Ireland.

This was just one of many clashes during the two-week hearing between the arguments for national security and those for the normal rules of open justice, but on this occasion at least we were partially successful. Having discussed the arguments, the magistrates agreed to a compromise: Lieutenant-Colonel A need not give his real name in open court, but it must be written down and handed to the defence. We would then know who, if nothing more, we were dealing with.

To the prosecution even this degree of openness was unacceptable. Michael Coombe, who had already attacked the integrity of one of our solicitors, was furious, and peevishly refused to allow the secretive A to appear. There followed a feverish search to find a substitute, and after consultations with the Ministry of Defence and the Director of Public Prosecutions the selectors homed in on Colonel B. It was agreed that there was absolutely nothing in his past career the revelation of which could jeopardize the national interest, but he must still remain anonymous to all but the lawyers and the three of us.

By the time the Colonel himself appeared at Tottenham Magistrates Court a few days later, an atmosphere of curiosity had therefore been created. Who was he, and what would he have to say? A tall, avuncular man with short, grey hair, a grey suit and a white handkerchief neatly folded in his breast pocket, the Colonel stood up straight in the witness box and waited for the questions.

Colonel B did not enjoy the experience of giving evidence one little bit. For two days he was asked to talk about a subject he had never publicly discussed before. There was some protection, he could see, in the fact that particular Sigint units were not identified, and there was reference only to page numbers in the transcript of my tape-recording, no direct quotes. To an outsider this only made the exercise more bizarre and obscure. But for the Colonel that wasn't enough: his very presence in a public place seemed to him a breach of national security.

With his caution and stiffness, the Colonel was hardly an impressive witness. Some questions directly related to Sigint he simply couldn't answer. To others he replied that they were not within his 'competence', or to do so would itself break the Official Secrets Act. His attitude towards secrecy on Sigint was so comprehensive that it even covered an opinion on how much money it cost to run, and with the backing of Michael Coombe he was stopped from saying whether any of the specific information on the tape was accurate, and therefore actually useful to this vaguely defined 'enemy'.

At times, his recital of the grave dangers that would result from publication of our interview sounded serious enough. With examples from the tape, he listed six categories of increasing damage to the organization. But was it really so secret, for instance, that there was a Sigint base on Cyprus, which everyone could see and talk about? 'Nobody in his right mind would bury an intercept station in a coal mine,' as the Colonel admitted himself in a rare moment of humour.

The prosecution was of course in a double bind. It wanted to make a public example of the three of us for delving too far. Yet the only people it could produce to support this case were those who had been told time and time again not to breathe a word about what they were doing. They merely confirmed the inward-looking vision of the secret society.

But though the Colonel stuck closely to his script and was reluctant to venture into any new territory, he did reveal one interesting piece of information. In answer to a question from Duncan Campbell's barrister, he agreed that his appointment to the Ministry of Defence had appeared, along with many others, in the *Wire*, the journal of the Royal Signals Association. To be precise, in the issue of December 1974.

The *Wire*, though technically on closed subscription, is available for anybody to read in a number of London libraries which keep back-copies. So it didn't take a genius in investigative journalism to check the relevant issue and discover that Colonel B did indeed have a real name – Hugh Anthony Johnstone MBE. Even his address and telephone number were listed in the London phone directory. If it was really that simple, then presumably the 'enemy' had done the same exercise many years before. All at once the identity of Colonel B was blown and the myth of national security exposed.

Just as the anonymous Colonel B had quickly become a symbol of the unnecessary secrecy surrounding our prosecution, so it was inevitable that his real name would be seen as a weapon with which to attack that system. It wasn't just his name, of course, but what he represented. Yet in the furore that eventually resulted from the naming of Johnstone, the secret world only emphasized its paranoia. However hard it tried, there was one thing it couldn't do: keep something as simple as a name quiet.

A month after the hearing at which we were committed for trial to the Old Bailey, the process started. Johnstone's name was printed in two radical magazines, *Peace News* and the *Leveller*, both active in opposition to the ABC case. *Peace News* argued that national security was being used to shroud Colonel B in unjustified anonymity. The *Leveller* asked simply: 'Who are you trying to kid, Colonel H. A. Johnstone?'[1] For both it was an act of defiance to the security authorities.

Perhaps worried at the fuss that was already surrounding the ABC case, it took them some time to react, but eventually they did. With the backing of the Attorney-General, Sam Silkin (the man who approved the ABC prosecution in the first place), the Director of Public Prosecutions moved slowly into action. Two Special Branch officers were dispatched to buy copies of the offending magazines. They then visited the offices of both publications in quick succession and interviewed members of

1. *Peace News*, 16.12.77; *Leveller*, 1.78.

their staffs. To each they carried the same message: they could be prosecuted for contempt of court in naming the Colonel.

Contempt of court is one of those areas, rather like that of official secrets, where reform has been promised for some time but never introduced. It is a constant problem for journalists reporting court cases, since it refers in the most general terms to any 'interference with the due administration of justice'. In this case the magazines were said to have ignored a 'direction' of the Tottenham magistrates to keep Johnstone's name secret. That there had never been any such order was only later confirmed, but at the time the prospect for two small magazines with limited resources was bleak: they now faced heavy legal costs and possible fines or imprisonment if found guilty.

But if the government's legal officers had expected to deter further publication of the name by this action, they were badly mistaken. A snowball effect had already begun, and around the country more small alternative magazines began to print Johnstone's name in explanations of the ABC case. He was mentioned during a discussion programme on Capital Radio and was mischievously paged at smart London hotels, though the BBC decided to cautiously bleep out the name from an interview on the *Today* programme with a member of the *Leveller*'s editorial group. To a casual listener this must have appeared rather like a silly joke, not the serious issue of national security it was supposed to be.

Since its members on the *Leveller* and *Peace News* were facing prosecution, the National Union of Journalists also became involved, and the name was published in the *Journalist*, the union's monthly newspaper. The *Journalist* had a circulation of 30,000, far higher than the other papers, and reached a wide readership among the profession. It too was visited by the Special Branch and warned of possible prosecution. But it wasn't until a busy week in April 1978 – exactly midway between our committal from the magistrates and our Old Bailey trial – that the security machine so overreacted that it caused a constitutional crisis. The 'Colonel B Affair', as it became nationally known, quickly developed into black comedy.

The initial reason for this was the annual conference of the NUJ, to be held in the coastal resort of Whitley Bay. For a week there would be discussions about new printing technology, the freedom of the press, wages and the closed shop. But among the long list of motions up for debate, there were several which both named Colonel B and condemned the threat of legal action against the three publications. When this fact was given advance publicity in the *Guardian* there was an immediate reaction.

In a letter to the union the Director of Public Prosecutions issued a thinly veiled threat. The NUJ must either stop any further disclosure of the name or face the consequences. That meant prosecution for contempt of court. A deadline was also set for lunchtime on the very same day that the letter was delivered. Nothing could have been more guaranteed to raise the temperature.

It was hardly surprising that the journalists' union, of which Duncan and myself were also members, would not accept what amounted to censorship of its internal proceedings. At a meeting of the union's executive, even those who were nervous of the possible legal consequences decided that the government's heavy-handed action should be fought. The deadline was ignored, the debate went ahead and I, as one of the few people who had actually seen Colonel B, explained why we had objected to his anonymity in the first place.

Having raised the stakes, however, the Director of Public Prosecutions then had to carry out his threat. Even as the debate was happening, two Special Branch officers,[1] who had driven up from Scotland Yard, waited nervously in the foyer of the conference hall to deliver the papers of prosecution on the union's General Secretary. When they were told that he was inside the conference, they hesitated. It didn't seem politically astute for the Special Branch to make such a public entrance. They handed their bundle to another union official and left. But their presence only emphasized the mixture of farce and secrecy that was fast developing.

Such was the atmosphere inside the conference itself that

1. Detective Sergeants Fickling and Shaw, both involved in the ABC investigation.

the following day two hundred delegates marched out of the hall, through the streets and assembled outside the police station where I was due to register my regular signature as a condition of bail. Just as my daily 'signing on' was a symbol of the petty restrictions imposed by the ABC case, so the spontaneous march reflected their anger at the Colonel B charade. The local police were amazed and Whitley Bay, a quiet seaside town, had never seen anything quite like it.

But there was still more to come. Incensed by the attempt to gag the NUJ conference, four MPs rose from their seats in the House of Commons the same afternoon and asked successive questions about reform of the Official Secrets Act. All of them incidentally referred to Johnstone by name. At first nobody realized what had happened, but as soon as the penny dropped there was uproar.

The implications of this were far more serious than a simple argument with the NUJ. According to long-established tradition the proceedings of parliament can be reported in their entirety, whatever is said. The debate was also being recorded by the broadcasting companies. And yet three publications were being prosecuted for doing precisely the same as the four MPs. A clash between the constitutional rights of parliament, the freedom of the press and the power of the courts became inevitable.

The Director of Public Prosecutions tried hard to stop this extraordinary escalation of the Colonel B affair. He sent an immediate statement over the Press Association wire service to all national newspapers and broadcasters. This warned them that they too could be prosecuted for contempt of court. In Fleet Street a decision had to be made: whether to publish, as they always had done, an accurate record of parliamentary business, or accept this outside pressure.

In the end, the advice was almost totally ignored. The Colonel's name was read out by Angela Rippon on BBC television and by Alastair Burnet on ITV, and was printed the following morning in nearly every daily newspaper. One paper managed a headline almost two inches high. 'Johnstone,' it read, 'the name only MPs may say.' Millions of people had been let into the secret that never really was.

For days afterwards, the argument about the rights and wrongs of the affair continued to occupy columns of newsprint. Were the MPs right to name the Colonel in parliament in the first place, should the Director of Public Prosecutions have intervened and what was this ABC case about anyway? There were jokes about Colonels X, Y and Z, and about the security services refusing to confirm or deny anything, however trivial. The very name Colonel B was soon synonymous with arbitrary secrecy.

But though the authorities had failed miserably in their efforts to keep Johnstone's identity under wraps, they refused to retire gracefully from the fray. Having decided, wisely, not to take on the combined forces of Fleet Street and national television, they still continued with the prosecution of the *Leveller*, *Peace News* and the *Journalist*, and the legal ramifications proved equally disastrous.

At the High Court, the three magazines argued that the Tottenham magistrates had never made a specific order banning publication – an argument confirmed by the clerk of the court himself – and that anyway Colonel B had given it all away in his evidence. As members of the Special Branch team which arrested us watched from the public gallery, the Lord Chief Justice, Lord Widgery, rejected their pleas. They were all found guilty of contempt of court and fined a total of £1,200.

Many months later, and well after the ABC trial itself, five learned peers sat in a wood-panelled room at the House of Lords and reconsidered this judgment. Without exception, they agreed with the magazines and disagreed with Lord Widgery. The fines, together with all their legal costs, were refunded. Justice, somewhat belatedly, was seen to be done, and contempt of court was shown as yet another weapon to be used by the security system to frustrate embarrassing revelations.

As the naming of Colonel B had displayed with breathtaking clarity, if there is one thing the secret world hates most it is publicity. It would far rather operate beneath the threshold of public consciousness where in turn the 'national security' is accepted as good and 'subversion' as bad, no questions asked.

With the ABC case it badly miscalculated. Not only did our arrest spark off a protest which lasted on and off for almost two years, but in the process those very questions that had lain dormant began to be asked. Who were the Special Branch and what were their powers? Why had a law which the government was committed to repeal been revived yet again against journalists? What really lay behind this obsession with secrecy? By the end, far more interest had been aroused about the inner workings of national security than can ever have been intended.

Right at the start, the ABC story was definitely news. It had intrigue, suspense and secrecy – and the added element that journalists themselves were in the firing-line. It was guaranteed to make the front pages. At nearly every appearance in court we were shadowed not only by the Special Branch but by the whirring of TV cameras. But as the saga dragged on, for weeks and then months, so the interest waned. ABC was overtaken by Jeremy Thorpe, the Grunwick dispute and rumours of a general election. Of the national papers only the *Guardian* followed closely what was happening behind the occasional, brief court hearings.

There were some good reasons for this, apart from the obvious search for new dramas and new scandals. What is news is not simply a matter of what happens, but a complicated mixture of the political and social judgements of individual editors. At the same time, the press can be hamstrung by the *sub judice* rule, which means that no comment is supposed to be made on a pending court case until its passage is completed. The rule can be useful in discouraging the hounding of people whose alleged crimes have already received wide coverage, but it can also stifle debate. Supporting an issue is again different from just reporting it, and there was widespread scepticism both about our broaching of 'genuine' secrets and about the fact that we worked for *Time Out*, a magazine whose anti-establishment position often cocks a snook at Fleet Street. We didn't accept the rules of the game, and the interview with John Berry was the most glaring evidence of this.

Such doubts were deliberately encouraged by the secret

agencies and, just as had happened in the Agee–Hosenball case, the rumours spread. At one stage, *Time Out* magazine was itself labelled as receiving funding from the Russians. But the most striking evidence of this was not revealed until over a year after our trial had finished, when the *New Statesman* published extracts from an internal memorandum prepared for a possible programme on London Weekend TV.[1] This four-page detailed briefing, written by researcher Gerry Gable, showed graphically how the security services had helped feed into the media a fictitiously sinister background to both the deportations and the ABC case.

The central character of the London Weekend memorandum was in fact Phil Kelly – the convenor of the Agee–Hosenball Defence Committee, a former *Time Out* writer and a strong supporter of the ABC Campaign. I have already mentioned the break-in to Kelly's car just before our arrest, a sign that he was of interest to the snoopers. But the briefing showed more pre-cisely what was being concocted around his position – evidently of central importance to the security services – as a key link between the protests at the deportation of the two Americans and at our own treatment. (Kelly has incidentally never been charged with any offence connected with these events.)

From basically accurate personal details, such as the fact that he then worked for a London-based news agency and his earlier involvement with the Young Liberals, a scenario was developed in which Kelly had travelled to Cuba for training in guerrilla warfare, learned about firearms and explosives from the Pale-stinians in Jordan and eventually become a KGB spy. But the document also encompassed the ABC case, alleging (from the writer's 'top level security sources') that for *four* years before our arrest a group of individuals, including John Berry and Duncan Campbell, had been 'systematically gathering top level security material'. Their leading light was again Phil Kelly – 'the KGB man who reaps the goodies'. None of these ridiculous assertions had any foundation.

Where then had Gerry Gable got his potentially damaging information? Though some of it, he says, came from people 'on

1. *New Statesman*, 15.2.80.

the left', a fair proportion was directly fed in by a security contact, probably in the Special Branch. There are several references in the text to 'security service' sources and also to an informer, who had infiltrated a number of groups and reported back, particularly on Kelly. 'I have now given the names I have acquired to be checked out by British/French security services . . .' the memorandum concluded. 'It is now a time of waiting for a feed-back and also further checks here.'

No television programme ever resulted from these investigations, perhaps partly because their most sensational aspects were untrue. But if the black propaganda being offered to Gable, and quite possibly to other journalists, was frightening enough, then the timing of this particular memorandum was equally critical. Written in May 1977 – at a time when the Attorney-General was still deliberating whether to give official sanction to our charges, the Special Branch were busily searching out 'harder' evidence, and the House of Commons was about to debate the issue of the deportations – it was crucial for the security services to spread as much dirt as they could. As his security contacts themselves told Gable, they felt 'that once the real nature of this [the ABC] case begins to emerge, they expect people like Jonathan Aitken [the Tory MP who spoke at an early ABC public meeting] will fade away fast.' The 'decent people', as they were described, would disappear.

Unfortunately for the security services, this didn't happen. For though the powerful and largely conservative national media were sometimes uncertain which way to jump, others weren't. Before long a small group of friends had become a long list of supporters, a network of groups around the country with one single aim: condemning the ABC prosecution. Members of Parliament, journalists, trade unionists, lawyers, civil servants – and hundreds of people who had never heard of us before – began to query what was going on. Together they made up what was inevitably known as the ABC Campaign.

The campaign tried hard to counter the secrecy and suspicion that automatically surrounded a case involving the Official Secrets Act. Thousands of leaflets were printed explaining who we were, what happened to us and why. Public meetings were called, petitions circulated demanding the dropping of the charges, and posters plastered around the capital. Much of this was aimed at dispelling the myths that had been created, often inadvertently, in the press, for instance that we had actually *written* an article rather than just talked. But the campaign also looked for more active support: MPs and prominent figures were lobbied, organizations and individuals asked to protest and to write letters to the politicians and the papers. Every week a small committee met in the traditional smoke-filled upstairs room of a pub to discuss tactics.

When publicity lapsed, the campaign worked to revive it. Our arrival at the Magistrates Court was invariably accompanied by a stunt. Children wore badges reading 'MI 3' or 'MI $5\frac{1}{2}$', depending on their age. A symbolic journalist was bound, gagged and seated behind a typewriter whose keys he couldn't touch, and when Colonel B appeared, a supporter dressed up in full military regalia and paraded through the streets at the head of a small procession. Though his uniform, hired from a theatrical costumier, was unfortunately that of another rank, he was still christened Colonel X.

Publicizing an issue on which 'Official Secret' was stamped in heavy red letters was never easy, however. The stunts were intended to attract the uncommitted in to the deeper arguments; but then everyone wanted to know what deadly secrets my tape-recorder cassettes contained. That was the one thing, on pain of losing our bail and going to prison, we couldn't talk about, and when we explained that the interview was not very dramatic and that it was the principle of the conversation which mattered to the authorities, the sceptical looks only increased. We became prisoners of our own fearful silence.

At times, the very powerlessness of the individual against the vast resources of the state only increased our pessimism about the outcome. We were always reacting to the latest outrageous development, never taking the initiative. Against the background of the surveillance of the Agee–Hosenball Committee, we wondered nervously at each meeting who was the police spy, a paranoia encouraged when the pub in which we met regularly was gutted by an unexplained fire-bomb attack. We had few resources, even less money and no influence within the establishment. It was all too tempting to just wait, hoping that with good lawyers, careful legal arguments and a sympathetic jury we would prove our innocence.

But gradually the anger and frustration felt by our closest supporters spread out. Dozens of people signed 'complicity statements' saying that they also had broken the Official Secrets Act, either as journalists or as government workers. Special forms were printed on which they could fill in the details of the information they had obtained or divulged, ranging from a minor leak of radioactivity at a power station to the procedure for stamping passports. Among the signatories were a journalist on *The Times* and a worker at the Bank of England. One reporter wrote that he had broken the law 'times without number' over the previous twenty years.

In parliament, although the actual case could not be raised directly (because of the *sub judice* rule), there were questions about the mysterious break-ins, the quizzing of Duncan Campbell's contacts and the activities of the Special Branch. As a result, for the first time, the number of officers employed in that secretive branch of the police was revealed.[1] Outside, numerous organizations, from local Labour Parties to trade unions to pressure groups, began to prepare their opposition to our arrest, and the NUJ in particular gave money and facilities. Meanwhile, a steady flow of articles and plugs appeared in student magazines, radical journals and the most unlikely corners of the commercial press. An anonymous group, the Campaign for the Revelation of Secret Information, sent round a duplicated bulletin on the activities of MI5 and MI6, clearly based on the inside knowledge of a 'whistleblower'.

Particular attention was given to the two politicians most closely involved, Merlyn Rees and Sam Silkin. At the Labour Party's annual conference, Rees was presented with a scale model of the London Post Office Tower, a photo of which appeared in the evidence against Duncan Campbell. He declined to accept this generous symbol of the prosecution's absurdity. Silkin was sent hundreds of signatures to a petition asking him

1. House of Commons, 24.5.78.

not to continue with the case, was questioned at public meetings and even found his own constituency party passing a resolution which, in guarded terms, suggested he should think again. That, in particular, was too close to home for comfort.

The campaign also benefited from a rising tide of demands for reform of the Official Secrets Act itself. This was one of the few pieces of legislation promised in the Labour Party Manifesto that had not been enacted, and a number of pressure groups, from Public Secrets to the Freedom of Information Campaign, were calling for a law much closer to the American model, with its statutory right of access to official files. The debate over their proposals formed a constant backcloth to the ABC case itself.

When the government finally published its own plans in the summer before our trial,[1] however, there was no change to Section 1, no commitment to freedom of information, whilst it proposed actually strengthening the law in the area of security. One part referred specifically to the dangers of the gradual accumulation of small items of information, a direct reflection of the separate charge against Duncan Campbell: the hand of the security services was plainly evident. Merlyn Rees described the changes somewhat ineptly as an armalite rifle to replace a blunderbuss, and said he hadn't touched Section 1 because that was the 'spy clause' – despite the fact that the prosecution in our case had already admitted we weren't spies. The reforms received almost universal criticism in the national press, the *Daily Mirror* labelling them 'Waste Paper' in an editorial.

Against the background of this controversy the ABC Campaign kept up its barrage of often humorous publicity. A cottage industry of badges, stickers and carrier bags carried the message into the most unlikely places. Every aspect of official secrecy was ridiculed. One badge read 'Tell Me Your Official Secrets', another 'I Am A Security Risk'. The most popular slogan of all pronounced with sinister satire: 'Buzby says: Who's Tapping Your Phone?' When the Post Office's advertising agents complained that its copyright had been breached in T-shirts bearing

1. In a White Paper, *Reform of Section 2 of the Official Secrets Act*. No legislation resulted before the Labour government was defeated in May 1979.

this message, the campaign replied tongue-in-cheek that it had consulted the little bird and he had given his permission. In fact, the Buzby sticker can still be found attached to many private and public phones.

Even the secret world itself did not escape the spotlight. On the anniversary of our arrest a tour was organized round London's secret landmarks. As a loudspeaker van explained what went on inside, we left slices of a giant imitation birthday cake at each of the five buildings, including the headquarters of MI5. It was a gentle reminder that they had not been forgotten.

After the fuss over the naming of Colonel B, interest in the case dramatically increased. At the campaign's tiny office the daily postbag doubled in size, bringing protests, offers of practical support – and donations. A full time organizer was employed. Around the country local ABC campaigns organized their own events, such as a sponsored walk round secret sites in Oxfordshire, and, most importantly, began to investigate the secret apparatus of their area. Several pamphlets were published describing local preparations by the state to deal with a major emergency. Every week one of the three of us was invited to speak at a public meeting, and by the time the trial approached the issue had been raised in scores of different ways.

Eventually, the campaign also took its protest to Cheltenham. On a sweltering summer day, as the tarmac melted in the road, several hundred people marched through the town from one GCHQ site to the other. Along the way a giant puppet of a judge banged the marchers on their heads with a gavel, a 'black ball' was delivered to the private club where Sir Leonard Hooper was a member and, at the end, a theatre group performed a special 'secrets' play. It was a typical ABC event – a mixture of humour and politics.

But as we stood outside the barbed wire of Britain's eavesdropping headquarters, the reality of our position was only too clear. From the rooftop two officials surveyed the march through binoculars. One of them carried a recording device. If the aim of the ABC Campaign had been to turn the tables and say, 'We're watching you', then there was little doubt that they were still watching us.

6

Twelve Good Men and Vetted

When the twelve members of the jury filed one by one into their seats in Court Number 1 at the Old Bailey, they looked an ordinary enough bunch. Alongside the suits and ties which we had worn for the occasion and the sober black gowns of the barristers, their clothes appeared encouragingly casual. There were some stern faces, but there were also some smiles. One of them, a long-haired man in jeans and cowboy boots, was even carrying a book by George Orwell, an author whose frightening creation of Big Brother was particularly appropriate.

To the three of us, locked in behind the solid glass panels of the grandiose dock, such first impressions seemed only too important. The jury was the one totally unknown factor in a case that was already heavily loaded in favour of the state. Only once in the last thirty years had any defendants pleaded not guilty to charges under Section 1 of the Official Secrets Act, and then unsuccessfully. If the jury could be persuaded to look at the facts, and ignore the prosecution's grave warnings of national disaster, then at least we stood a chance. It was therefore worth studying their attitudes, their expressions, any hint of what they might be thinking.

But there was one essential piece of information about the jury which their appearance did not give away. They themselves were not even aware of it. This was that every single one of them had been processed by the very same Special Branch which had pursued our case with such determination. Well before the trial had even started, they had been monitored against Special Branch files, assessed for their 'loyalty' and checked for 'extreme political beliefs'. How the Branch can interpret such a phrase has already been seen. In effect, it meant that the organization which arrested us, carried out the investigations and interviewed witnesses was now scrutinizing the people who would decide our guilt or innocence. It was an extraordinary attack on the right to a fair trial.

This discovery, that the security services had even penetrated the supposedly inviolate sanctuary of the jury, was only the first of many surprises during the ABC trial, itself the culmination of almost two years of controversy and legal wrangles. But if it exposed in stark form the sheer power of the agencies of national security, then the controversy about the issue also followed what was to become a familiar pattern during the two-month court case. Against the power of the Official Secrets Act and the secrecy that it protected was set the determination of the ABC campaigners, our legal advisers and a number of sympathetic reporters to burst the bubble of the spying slur, a strength of feeling which had steadily built up over the preceding months. The more a veil of secrecy was thrown over the proceedings, the more everyone wanted to know what was happening underneath. Before describing the trial itself, it is therefore worth explaining how this initial argument about jury vetting unfolded, and has since developed into a continuing political debate.

In fact it was only by chance, on that very first day of the trial, that we discovered the jury had been vetted. During a casual conversation with one of the court officials, one of our barristers was told that the prosecution had secretly applied for a list of all eighty-two members of the panel from whom the eventual twelve jurors were selected. All this had happened six weeks before the hearing began; we had never been told. When we protested, it was found that eleven of those eighty-two were not in court. Had *they* been picked out in the vetting process as disloyal, or subversive, or unreliable? The prosecutor's assurances that their absence was not his doing, that jury checks were common 'in cases of this kind', and that none of the potential jurors had in fact been disqualified as a result, hardly diminished our suspicion.

From those brief and inadequate details given in court, a controversy quickly developed outside among both lawyers and the press. Perhaps naively, it had generally been assumed that jurors were chosen at random from the lists, kept by every local council, of those eligible to vote in elections. Nobody, including the prosecution, knew anything about them apart from their names and addresses. They could be challenged in court, and replaced by another member of the panel, but normally just on their appearance. Yet here was evidence not only that they'd been extensively investigated but that the state maintained the right to exclude any of them it didn't like. It wasn't so much jury vetting as jury rigging.

As the speculation increased, and, as we shall see later, the composition of the jury continued to remain at the centre of the ABC trial, so the politicians felt bound to react. Eventually, the Attorney-General, Sam Silkin, issued a statement to the press[1] – a response, as he put it, to 'inaccurate statements which have appeared in certain periodicals'. This provided both a rare glimpse inside the world of national security and the first official admission that jury vetting was a long-standing and regular practice.

Silkin explained that he had first learned of its extent in 1974, and had decided then to issue guidelines to police and prosecutors. These guidelines, published as part of his statement, allowed checks against police records in the case of any 'serious offences where strong political motives' were involved, including trials under the Official Secrets Act. The ABC case apart, vetting had been used in no less than twenty-three trials in the previous three years, and in over half there had been checks with the Special Branch. Applications for the list of potential jurors by the prosecution had also, as in our trial, invariably been made without the knowledge of the defence.

The purpose of these checks, according to the Attorney-General, was 'to forestall, in the interests of justice, the presence on a jury of a person when, and only when, there is very good reason to believe that he may be incapable of coming to a true verdict, or to maintain secrecy according to the law, by reason of extreme views or susceptibility to improper pressure.' That a 'true verdict' was supposed to be the jury's unhindered task, whatever its prejudices, and that majority verdicts had already allowed for the presence of oddballs seemed irrelevant to the

1. Published in *The Times*, 11.10.78, mid-way through the ABC trial, and reprinted in *Justice Deserted: The Subversion of the Jury* (NCCL, 1979).

state's determination to keep out 'troublemakers'. But, most importantly, these guidelines under which jury vetting was carried out had, until then, been totally secret and had no basis in law.

If Silkin had hoped to defuse the public debate by openly publishing these guidelines, then he was rapidly proved wrong. Jury vetting has since become a major political and legal issue. Historically, it raised spectres of the literal packing of juries with its supporters by the Crown, which had been common in the early nineteenth century. In a stinging attack on Silkin's guidelines,[1] written in the polemical style of that time to avoid contempt of court, the historian E. P. Thompson pointed out the embarrassing parallels and asked: 'What kind of people are we that the state should have an independent power to pry furtively into our most private affairs while its own affairs are screened from us as Official Secrets?'

Vetting was also interpreted as just one of a series of more recent attacks on the right to trial by jury, not least of which was the reduction in the number of challenges a defendant could make as the jurors appear in court. In 1977, this was reduced from seven to three. And there was the important element of the information itself, on the basis of which the police could request the exclusion of a juror. If the Special Branch was involved, this was certain to include details of their political views.

Since the ABC trial, an increasing number of jury vetting cases have come to light, sometimes totally outside the type of prosecutions listed in Silkin's guidelines. (In Northamptonshire, for instance, the police were found to have been checking criminal records of *all* potential jurors, a system which Silkin's successor, Sir Michael Havers, roundly condemned.) The most dramatic of these involved the case of six people charged with conspiracy to rob, all of whom were said to be anarchists.[2] Well before their trial started it was discovered that the ninety-three members of the jury panel had been vetted. They had been checked not only with the Special Branch but with central

1. *New Society*, 19.10.78.
2. Four of the six, in what was called the 'Persons Unknown' case, were eventually acquitted in December 1979.

criminal records and local police. But when the raw results of some of those checks were reported in the *Guardian*, there was an even greater outcry.[1]

Information obtained from police files on nineteen of the potential jurors covered a frighteningly wide range. One man was listed as living at an 'address believed to be a squat'. Another had made a complaint against the police, though it was later withdrawn. Others had merely been the victims of crimes or had close associations with criminals, though a 'criminal' didn't necessarily mean someone who had been actually convicted of a crime. A handful had genuine convictions, some of which were so old that they had legally expired under the Rehabilitation of Offenders Act and could therefore have easily been expunged from the records. Even without any vetting, such details could be useful to a prosecution lawyer wanting to push a particular point.

This unique exposure of the actual results of a jury vetting raised the debate to an entirely new level and once more brought Silkin's guidelines into the limelight. According to his statement during the ABC trial, the defence should also be given some of the information obtained from checking jurors' police records, though we had never been told a thing. Yet although the defence in the 'anarchists' trial *was* given the details published in the *Guardian*, this quite clearly did not include the type of political background on individuals kept by the Special Branch. Such evidence of allegedly 'extreme political beliefs' from the Branch was likely to be the most crucial in a decision to exclude a juror, but it was obviously considered too sensitive to pass on.

At the same time, the guidelines pointed out that the defence could carry out its own investigation of the jury panel, and the anarchists were eventually allowed a limited amount of public money for this purpose. Without the resources of police files or those of other state departments, however, this was an impossible exercise, and it also involved exactly the same intrusion into people's private lives that vetting had raised as an issue. Both these arguments only underlined the ludicrous nature of Silkin's attempt to open out, and equalize, a system which, as the

1. *Guardian*, 20.9.79. The reporter, David Leigh, was later given a British Press Award for his articles on jury vetting.

Sunday Times put it, 'offers a gross advantage to the prosecution'.[1]

In the aftermath of the *Guardian*'s disclosures there were renewed demands for a system of completely random selection of juries. The *Daily Mail*'s legal correspondent, Fenton Bresler, for example, wrote that a series of measures, including jury vetting, meant that 'we are in danger of creating a climate of thought where the jury ceases to be regarded as the essential linchpin of our system of criminal justice'. The trial judge himself, Alan King-Hamilton, refused to accept these criticisms, strongly criticized a television programme for discussing them and ordered a new jury to be vetted.

Since then, there has been a continuing controversy in which the police have called for jury vetting in all court cases, whereas the judiciary has begun to realize its dangers for civil liberties. Lord Denning, voicing his objection to vetting in a case in which two policemen were themselves accused, said: 'So long as a person is eligible for jury service I cannot think it is right that behind his back, the police should go through his record so as to enable him to be asked to "stand by" for the Crown or to be challenged by the defence. If this sort of thing is to be allowed, what becomes of a man's right to privacy?'[2] The politicians, in the middle, have so far shown no inclination to radically change the system, despite two private members' bills aimed at outlawing the practice.

Most dramatically, in the middle of this controversy, Sam Silkin admitted that he had issued his guidelines on vetting against a background of pressure for no juries at all in 'political' cases. There was little doubt that the pressure had come from the security services. There is equally little doubt that without the ABC trial, and without Silkin's admission that the practice was officially approved, jury vetting would have remained a secret and largely unchallenged process.

Jury vetting was, as I have already explained, just the first of

1. *Sunday Times*, 23.12.79.
2. Court of Appeal, 3.3.80. A later Appeal Court ruling in June 1980 decided that vetting was 'not unlawful'.

several examples of the power of the security system to emerge during the ABC trial. But even before those twelve jurors made their dramatic appearance it was obvious that the trial would be, for us, an uphill struggle. Every feature of the legal defence was surrounded by secrecy and security. We had of course done some preparation, and Duncan Campbell in particular had unearthed an enormous amount of material from public sources. But there was no certainty that any of it, under the oppressive terms of Section 1 of the Official Secrets Act, would be admissible in open court. Section 1 permitted, for instance, secret, *in camera*, hearings and, as a result of a House of Lords ruling, allowed the state to decide itself what is or isn't an official secret.

At first, the transcript of our conversation was itself considered so sensitive – with a 'Top Secret' stamp on every page – that our lawyers could view it only at Scotland Yard. When eventually they were given copies, these still had to be locked up every night in a safe. One barrister had to buy one specially for the occasion.

We had also discovered our own technical expert to argue against the opinions of Colonel B. He was a well-known professor, John Erikson, from Edinburgh University, a specialist in communications information theory and the acknowledged Western expert on Soviet military strategy. Erikson had actually done research for the Ministry of Defence and was outraged at the labelling of our interview as Top Secret. But whereas the Colonel had been allowed to remain anonymous, the security services made sure that *our* adviser was thoroughly investigated: his name had to be forwarded to them for checking. As the Director of Public Prosecutions himself commented dryly to my solitor, Bill Nash: 'I think you and I both have very difficult clients in this matter.' Just before the trial, we were told that yet another anonymous prosecution witness, a 'Mr C', might appear.

The tone of the prosecution had equally been set by the approach of Michael Coombe, leading counsel at our committal hearing, who described Duncan Campbell as 'a thoroughly subversive man' and alleged, to wide press coverage, that our conversation could have put 'lives in Northern Ireland' at risk.

There was never any tenable support for this emotional impli-
cation – after all, John Berry had served in Cyprus – and it
failed to resurface at our trial.

In this situation the attitude of the judge would obviously be
important, and some indication of how the judiciary might
approach the case had already emerged from an application by
myself and John Berry for relaxation of our bail conditions. This
was heard by Mr Justice Melford Stevenson, whom I was asking
in particular for the return of my passport so that I could have a
holiday in France. But despite the fact that I had been invited
personally by a barrister, and there had never been any suggestion that any of us might abscond, Stevenson rejected the
application. Clearly impressed by the aura of 'national security',
he commented sarcastically: 'Why does he need to go on holiday
in France, unless he's particularly fond of garlic?'

At first, the trial judge himself was to be Mr Justice Thesiger,
a noted hard-liner with a record of heavy sentences. When
Thesiger fortuitously fell ill before the trial could start, he was
replaced by Mr Justice Willis. He at least had no reputation for
harshness, but he had, according to his entry in *Who's Who*, been
a one-time member of the Royal Corps of Signals.

Only one incident suggested any chink in the prosecution's
armour. Two months before the trial a meeting took place
between the defence and prosecution barristers. As a result of
this we were offered what is normally called a 'plea bargain'.
The terms of the bargain were that if we pleaded guilty to the
lesser Section 2 offences, then the more serious Section 1 charges
would be dropped. Even so, there was no guarantee on what
sentences we would receive, and there would be a permanent
injunction on Duncan using some of his research material, a
crude form of censorship.

Such deals are only too common behind the scenes of court
cases and rarely receive any publicity. For John Berry especially
it was a difficult choice. But after lengthy discussions about the
advantages and disadvantages we decided that we would all
continue to fight the prosecution all the way. The deal was a sign
of weakness, a cynical move which we should exploit. At a press
conference just before the trial we revealed its details. Some of

our lawyers were distinctly unhappy with this breach of their internal code of conduct.

So it was in an atmosphere of mutual suspicion that the two sides lined up at the Old Bailey in September 1978. Outside, a crowd of two hundred people carried placards and messages of protest, and a special 'souvenir' programme lampooning the trial was distributed. Inside, in the cold, air-conditioned cloister of Court Number 1, it was quieter but no less tense. Behind the three prosecution barristers sat seven advisers, including a man from GCHQ. Even the Director of Public Prosecutions was there. A team of Special Branch officers guarded the evidence, and in the middle, on a table, was a large tape-recorder waiting to play the crucial recording. Wires snaked away from it to a series of headphones: the court had literally been wired up.

For several days the chief prosecutor, John Leonard – a short, dapper man who had replaced the somewhat bumbling Michael Coombe – portrayed in carefully suggestive terms the details of our alleged crimes. (With the addition of two alternative charges against myself, we now faced a total of nine counts.) We weren't spies, agents of a foreign power, he said, but we had talked about matters we knew were prohibited from the public arena. The 'enemy' might know all the information we had discussed, but that didn't matter. They would be getting confirmation from the horse's mouth, John Berry. And that enemy wasn't just the Russians, but any country with which Britain might at some stage be in conflict.

The sensitivity of the information being described was constantly emphasized. When specific places or organizations were referred to, even in newspaper articles, their names were carefully blanked out. Photos were labelled only by numbers, and when it came to the playing of the tape, the court was cleared, the doors were firmly locked and the press and public were left to study sinister notices which read 'Court in Camera. No Admittance.' On the inside, as the barristers and the judge removed their wigs, donned their headphones and listened to our rambling interview, the court-room took on the appearance of some strange religious seance. The Special Branch, prowling its perimeter, were the high priests.

However, there was one item that stood out from the prosecution's lengthy catalogue as patently unreasonable. This was the separate charge against Duncan Campbell. He was said to have 'collected information on defence communications', including letters, pictures, notes and a card index; and yet collecting information was exactly what a good journalist *should* do. Even John Leonard had to admit that most of the hundreds of papers and photographs taken from Duncan's flat came from public sources. Again that didn't matter: it was the 'jigsaw puzzle' he had put together which was dangerous. In effect, it was being argued that if you matched two pieces of public information together and came up with something new, you could magically conjure up a secret.

This was clearly a fruitful subject for ridicule, and as the prosecution witnesses began to give their evidence, so Duncan's barrister, Jeremy Hutchinson, launched his counter-attack. Hutchinson was the most senior and experienced of the defence legal team, he had already been involved in one successful battle against the Official Secrets Act – the acquittal of Jonathan Aitken and the *Sunday Telegraph* in 1971[1] – and his quiet, elegant and persistent manner impressed the judge. Against the mass of supposedly dangerous material collected by Duncan he had one simple argument: how could these places be so secret when you could see them, walk past them and read about what they did in countless newspaper articles.

The witnesses in fact proved to be the security system's worst enemies. From a series of RAF officers came exactly the same tight-lipped refusal to answer questions that had made Colonel B so notorious. They had been called to give evidence about photographs of various military sites, but in some cases they had simply no idea about what went on inside the perimeter fences. Faced with a barrage of newspaper cuttings, official maps and publications which told them this information, they retreated behind the 'need to know' principle. One Wing Commander

1. The newspaper published parts of an allegedly secret report on British military aid to the Nigerian government. See *Officially Secret* by Jonathan Aitken (Weidenfeld and Nicolson, 1971).

finally agreed that the contrast between his own enforced silence and public comment was 'absolutely idiotic'.

The most extraordinary witnesses were a student from the Roman Catholic public school, Ampleforth College, and his form master, a Father Anselm Kramer. Why were this unlikely couple there? Simply because they had corresponded with Duncan Campbell about how they themselves might investigate the series of Post Office microwave towers which prominently dot the countryside. Like Campbell, they were intrigued by the possible defence uses of this apparently civilian network, and using a compass and a method described in a Penguin book[1] they had actually gone on a two-week trip around Scotland and the north-east of England following these towers from one to another. Kramer expressed genuine concern about whether this system was in fact to do with defence against a nuclear attack, and saw nothing wrong with his inquiries. But, unlike Campbell, he was not in the dock.

Despite attempts by the prosecution and the judge to cut short Hutchinson's protracted cross-examination of these witnesses, his persistent assault on what he called 'this bogus secrecy' continued. Gradually, the list of fifty-two secret sites prepared by the prosecution began to look thinner and thinner. Photos of them had appeared in the *Sunday Times*, there had been comments about their operations in dozens of official and unofficial publications, and one of them, the Post Office Tower in London, was a national landmark. Nothing could be more absurd than to pretend that was secret.

But what was the jury's reaction to this head-on clash between secrecy and the public's right to know? As the trial reached the end of its second week, it became obvious that there was more to those twelve silent faces than the fact that they had been vetted. Yet again, a series of incidents brought the position of the jury into dramatic prominence.

The first sign that there were at least some members of the jury who were already prepared to accept the prosecution line against us came just as my tape-recording was about to be played.

1. *Beneath the City Streets* by Peter Laurie (1972).

A note was passed to the judge explaining that several of them had themselves signed the Official Secrets Act. They were worried that, by listening to such secret material, they would be breaking their own binding commitments. The judge assured them that everybody who listened to the tape was anyway covered by an automatic bond of silence.

Our obvious fear that these individuals would hardly feel sympathetic towards our position was only confirmed when, after an inquiry by the judge, we were told how they had come to be covered by the Act. One worked in the civil service, another had been a squadron security clerk in the Army, but the third, and most important, had for many years served in the highly secretive Special Air Services regiment.

Whatever one's view of the SAS, it is certainly no ordinary Army unit. It specializes in undercover operations and has been closely associated with the work of MI6, Britain's overseas intelligence organization. A close-knit, elite force, its aggressive motto is 'Who Dares, Wins' and it has a reputation for exactly the type of activities – sabotage, interrogation, spying and guerrilla warfare – over which a shroud is officially placed. The juror had even been stationed at one time in Cyprus, where John Berry had served. How could a man with that background treat our case with any impartiality?

But there was another, equally vital, element to this discovery, for the ex-SAS officer wasn't just an ordinary member of the jury. He was its foreman, a central figure in any deliberations about the case. He had himself volunteered for that job and had made it clear, as it emerged afterwards, that he had no doubt at all about our guilt. Much of his time had been spent persuading the other jurors round to his point of view, and John Berry, he considered, should have been given a military trial and sentenced to fourteen years straight off. 'He never stopped talking about it, even in the corridors and in the canteen during lunch breaks, on and on, trying to convince the other members,' a fellow juror told the *New Statesman*.

Against the background of jury vetting, this was an even more alarming development. Though there was no evidence at all that the man had been planted, he was not going to help our chances of a fair trial; and while the jury was out of court our barristers made a strong objection to his presence. It wasn't only his likely prejudice, we argued, but his close connection to the issues of the trial. Duncan Campbell had even written a recent article which was distinctly uncomplimentary about the SAS. But the judge remained unmoved: the trial would continue, he ruled, and no reports of what had just been discussed must appear in the press. Though he didn't say so, such a report could amount to contempt of court.

As the Colonel B case had shown only too clearly, contempt of court is a legal minefield for journalists. Even the judges themselves couldn't agree about it. But whatever the rights and wrongs, there is one basic rule about court reporting, and that is that discussions held in the absence of the jury are not supposed to be published until the end of the trial. In the atmosphere of the ABC case, it was equally predictable that this rule would be broken.

Right from the start, reporting the ABC trial had not been easy. All journalists had been forced to apply for special passes before they even entered the court. They had then been presented with a largely obscure debate in which the most important factual elements – names of people and places – were deliberately omitted. For hours they were totally excluded from the court while even more secret matters were discussed. So, against that background, it was inevitable that any indiscretion, any slip of the tongue which revealed a 'secret' name, any issue of controversy, would be seized upon eagerly.

Throughout the first two weeks the temperature of controversy surrounding the case had also been steadily rising, encouraged in part by the ABC Campaign, which had even produced special 'ABC Are Innocent' badges. The BBC's *Nationwide* programme had run a humorous item about the trial's 'silly' secrets, especially the Post Office Tower. Most of the national press had carried long reports, some including thinly disguised comment. In Brighton, a heated argument developed at the annual Trade Union Congress over whether or not the case could be debated while the trial was in progress, and a Cabinet Minister, Tony Benn, had openly attacked 'national security' as a 'blanket excuse for secrecy on any matter which the government wants to conceal from public scrutiny'. Official secrecy was definitely in the news.

The existence of the SAS foreman of the jury added another element to that controversy. On the very next day after we had objected to him in court, the details of that objection were revealed on the TV chat show *Saturday Night People*, hosted by Russell Harty. The item lasted only a few seconds and was billed as the sort of news 'you won't have read anywhere else', but among the millions of viewers was the SAS man himself.

Whether the TV show had broken the law or not, it had an immediate effect. The following Monday, just as the trial was about to resume, the jury foreman informed the judge that he considered it to have prejudiced the hearing. The SAS man was clearly angry, but the judge was furious. He demanded to see a videotape of the programme, and for five solid hours there was pandemonium as lawyers bustled around the Old Bailey corridors attempting to disentangle the mess.

Eventually, the judge decided that he had only one choice. He would have to stop the trial and start again. 'I find it quite lamentable,' he announced in the sternest of voices, 'that the trial of a very serious matter in this court should be halted and public money thrown away because of a piece of gratuitous journalistic gossip.'

That, of course, though widely quoted, was a simplification, for the programme had done no more than repeat in shortened form the same arguments we had put in court. But the three of us were hardly displeased. Like Colonel B six months before, the stopping of the trial after only a fortnight was front page news. 'Harty Chat Show Stops Trial', screamed the *Daily Mirror*. Even the historic peace agreement between the Israelis and the Egyptians took second place in the popular press.

But as the controversy continued, over why three legal advisers had allowed the programme to go ahead and whether it was in fact contempt of court, there were other important developments. The judge, Mr Justice Willis, who had been moved to another trial, was suddenly taken ill and rushed to hospital. As a result, the date set aside for our new trial had to be delayed for another week.

During the breathing-space caused by this additional complication, the prosecution had time to assess their position, and in the end they came to one inescapable conclusion. Given the evidence produced so far, they would have to abandon the separate charge against Duncan Campbell of 'collecting information'. This was the first firm indication that the trial was becoming a severe embarrassment to them. So, as the court reassembled at the beginning of October for the second round, we had not only a new judge and a new jury but also a simple slogan: 'One charge down, eight to go'.

At first it appeared that this unexpected second ABC trial would be a tedious action replay. The prosecutor would again recite his grave indictment of our crimes, the court would be sealed off yet again while we listened to our three-hour conversation, and more security witnesses would refuse to answer questions about their work. If things went well, we would also prove from documents and press cuttings that they had been unnecessarily cautious. But there were of course two new elements – the judge and the jury.

The judge was Mr Justice Mars-Jones, a 65-year-old Welshman and a considerably tougher individual than his now invalid predecessor. Mars-Jones was determined from the start that there would be no repetition of the Russell Harty debacle. The jury was told to report any untoward approaches immediately and the press were warned against reporting anything said in their absence. The atmosphere became so tense that even a casual wink from one of the jurors to a journalist seated nearby was reported to the judge. But Mars-Jones was also keenly aware that there was something unusual about the use of spying charges against two journalists and their source. This realization, unspoken at first, eventually proved crucial.

As for the jury, they had again been vetted for their 'loyalty' by the security services, and again we were disarmed by the prosecution's assurance that none of them had been weeded out as a result. But this time we were also ready with our protests. Jeremy Hutchinson described the vetting as a 'secret and unconstitutional process' during a fervent and eloquent speech. 'To subject citizens to surveillance, to run their names through an MI5 computer, and then on undisclosed criteria via hidden methods pronounce upon their loyalty, is in my submission to strike at the very heart of the jury system,' he pronounced. Unfortunately, because the jury was not in court, this couldn't be reported.

Two concessions *were* made on the jury's selection. The defence was also handed a list of the jury panel and their addresses, though without the expense of private inquiry agents we had no hope of discovering anything important. We were also allowed to ask each juror a simple question as they were sworn in. Had they in the last fifteen years worked in a job where they handled secret material? It was intended partly to avoid another SAS man; one juror answered yes, and was excused.

There was also a new note of generosity towards the defence in the approach of the state prosecutor, John Leonard. He paid tribute to the profession of journalism as a defender of liberty and spent some time arguing that the much publicized reforms of the Official Secrets Act would not affect our trial – though on the surface at least they would have done. When it came to the 'Top Secret' tape-recording, he was persuaded to read out almost a quarter of its contents, stopping only when he reached what he called 'real secrets'. But his most telling remark was when he described the tape as containing 'matters which I'm told are secret'.

In fact, he had every reason to be worried. For just as the first trial had displayed the security services' paranoia about the information Duncan had collected, so the second exposed the same contradiction about Signals Intelligence, the subject of our interview with John Berry.

To the prosecution, the places and units we had discussed were so secret that they had to be given letters and numbers in court rather than names. A growing list of these codes, which each new witness had to learn, was a constant source of amusement and confusion. But as the witnesses appeared, they were taken by the defence through a long series of extracts from two openly available military publications. These were the *Wire*, the journal of the Royal Signals Association (where Colonel B's real name had been published), and the *Rose and Laurel*, the journal of the Intelligence Corps. From their pages it was possible to deduce an enormous amount about Sigint, and as the *Rose and Laurel* itself commented humorously: 'The journal is read by all sorts of people all over the world, including the K G B.'

At one point, having listened to these extracts, even the judge was forced to agree that 9th Signals Regiment in Cyprus, up till then known as Unit A at Location 1, could now be called by its proper name. But the prosecution, sensing the collapse of its carefully constructed system, immediately objected. There followed a full day's scurrying behind the scenes: the government was consulted, the Director of Public Prosecutions was called in, and after a secret statement from John Leonard, in which he outlined the security objections, Unit A returned to its original anonymity. The power of national security over the court, and the patent absurdity of keeping quiet a name everybody now knew, could hardly have been better displayed.

However, this proved only a temporary setback for the defence arguments. It was impossible to escape the fact that the very publications which the Royal Signals and Intelligence Corps put out were a valuable source of just the sort of information we were charged with discussing. The more the military witnesses refused to comment, and the more they described even published information as classified, the more ridiculous the prosecution looked.

By the time Colonel B reappeared, this time called by his real name, those arguments had been refined to their essentials. For several days, the Colonel was forced to carry out precisely the same sort of intelligence operation his 'enemies' might have performed. The only difference was that it involved no spying, merely a careful analysis of published sources. From those Army magazines themselves it was possible to discover where Sigint units were based, how many people worked there and the fact that they cooperated with other agencies, especially the Americans. Yet that was exactly the type of information we had discussed and the revelation of which Johnstone found so dangerous. When he described a letter written to the *Wire* as itself a breach of the Official Secrets Act, the secrecy had come full circle: it was attacking itself. 'To be frank,' he said at one stage, 'I am not certain what is a secret and what isn't.' Even the judge told Johnstone that the most serious allegations against us seemed 'hardly of earth-shattering importance'.

The press, who had to sit through this extraordinary exercise, would probably have agreed. But if there was little of substance to report inside the court, then there was plenty of room for speculation – and comment – outside.

As soon as the first trial was stopped, there were demands from MPs and others to the Attorney-General, Sam Silkin, to halt the entire proceedings. The whole issue of the Official Secrets Act had also reached boiling point: the Labour Party conference was calling for a British Freedom of Information law, one of the main civil service unions had supported us publicly, and even an eminent judge, Lord Scarman, had attacked the government's timid reform of the existing law.[1] While the ABC Campaign maintained its weekly vigil across the road from the Old Bailey, an almost daily collection of press cuttings, many potentially in contempt of court, was handed up to Mr Justice Mars-Jones. 'It looks as though the press is trying to make up my mind for me,' he commented sardonically.

What *was* in Mars-Jones's mind soon became apparent. He had already indicated briefly his concern about the use of Section 1 charges, and immediately after Colonel Johnstone had finished he asked to hear the legal arguments for and against. But these were quickly cut short by a simple, clear statement from the judge which could not have been misunderstood. Section 1 was about spying and sabotage, he said, and to use it otherwise raised important constitutional issues. 'The Attorney-General,' he concluded, 'has the power to start a prosecution. He also has the power to stop it.'

For Sam Silkin that was the end of the road. The following morning the prosecutor, having talked to Silkin, returned to court with his instructions. He had taken the judge's remarks to

1. In a speech to the Royal Institute of Public Administration, 10.10.78.

heart, and announced that the four most important charges, those which carried up to fourteen years in prison, those which we had feared most, would be dropped. When the jury was told of this decision, the judge, clearly pleased with his efforts, made a remark which must have echoed through the corridors of GCHQ: 'We now have to decide how many of the documents before you can be put on the bonfire.'

To the three of us it certainly seemed like a Guy Fawkes' night. This was the moment we had been waiting for: after over a year of tense anticipation, the smear of the spying charges had been suddenly swept away. The views of Colonel B had been finally discredited, and, at least temporarily, the secret world was in retreat. Though we had all been soberly imbued with the court tradition of respectful silence, we inwardly cheered. John Berry heaved the biggest sigh of relief in his life.

Outside the court, as the news was announced, there was jubilation. A crowd of supporters had already gathered for the weekly picket. There was a giant puppet in the shape of a dragon, representing the ogre of secrecy, there were children with placards and balloons, and in the middle were the press and television reporters, wanting to know why this extraordinary turn-around had occurred.

Why indeed? The judge had said that he had taken no notice of what he called the 'improper pressures' from the media and the Campaign. He had also not mentioned the cumulative effect of the defence cross-examination in exposing the myth of secrecy. However, it was more than interesting that he had used exactly the same argument which the ABC Campaign had advanced ever since we were first charged: that the use of Section 1 was, in his own words, 'oppressive'.

But there was one piece of information, equally important, which we could not – again because it had been given in the absence of the jury – say anything about. This was a promise from the judge, in terms as clear as his 'instruction' to Sam Silkin, that none of us, whatever happened in the rest of the trial, would go to prison. For the prosecution, that was the final rebuff. John Berry remarked that he would now, for the first time, be able to think about Christmas.

The collapse of the ABC trial was by then almost complete. Out of nine original charges only four remained, all of them under the less serious Section 2 of the Official Secrets Act. Revelation of our interview, previously judged so serious that it could be 'useful to an enemy', was now just embarrassing. And we were accused of breaking a part of the law which was so discredited that the last judge considering its use against journalists had said it should be pensioned off.[1]

Unfortunately that hadn't happened. Eight years later, despite countless demands for its reform from across the political spectrum, Section 2 still survived. Under its provisions, if a 'servant of the Crown' had even a discussion with you about his work, outside the official channels, you would both be guilty of an offence. It didn't matter whether what you talked about was classified or not. Section 2 had often been called a 'catch-all' law, and it was broken by journalists every day of the week, but it was still available to achieve a short, sharp conviction against those the authorities didn't like.

But if the judge had hoped by his announcement on sentences to persuade us to plead guilty to these lesser charges, he was mistaken. By the time the court resumed after a day's break, we were all still firmly in the 'not guilty' camp. We were on to a winning streak, and we were not going to stop now. The trial in fact lasted for a further three weeks, and it was the jury again which brought it to its cliff-hanging conclusion.

Meanwhile, there was one more small concession from Mr Justice Mars-Jones. He decided that one of the alternative charges against me was unsatisfactory legally. This had nothing to do with the central issues of the trial, but to the prosecution's annoyance they were still forced to drop it. To the press, however, this was 'Another Secrets Charge Dropped', and as the publicity continued, with protests outside the court and even a coincidental leading article in the *Guardian* attacking Section 2, the judge became more irritated by these attempts to 'usurp' his power.

Every time a new example of what he saw as unnecessary

---

1. Mr Justice Caulfield in the 1971 *Sunday Telegraph* trial.

comment on the trial was brought to his attention – whether a
newspaper article or a Campaign leaflet – he delivered a sharp
rebuke to its perpetrators. For instance, immediately after the
collapse of the Section 1 charges I had been interviewed on
ITV's *News at Ten* programme about my reaction. Learning of
this, Mars-Jones asked to see a replay of the bulletin and I
nervously brought in my toothbrush the next morning, expecting
that I might lose my bail. Fortunately I didn't. On another
occasion he spotted an ABC supporter in the public gallery
wearing a Buzby T-shirt – the man was asked quietly to cover it
up. Eventually, all three of us were ordered to have no contact
whatsoever with the press.

The most striking example was when a court official was called
to give evidence on oath that he had seen us talking to demonstrators outside the Old Bailey – and without the solicitor who
was supposed to accompany us everywhere when the trial was
not in session. Again fortunately, the man had made a mistake,
but the judge still threatened to send us to prison for the
remainder of the trial. 'I am determined to stop them seeing the
demonstrators just as much as I am determined to stop the
demonstrations,' he warned, even complaining that my wife,
Sue, was among them. In fact, Sue was one of the linchpins of
the ABC Campaign and had spent the previous few months
working in the Campaign's office. The following week, there was
an ironic display of blank placards. It's hard to describe both the
tension which built up as the trial progressed from one drama
to another and the determination of our supporters, whatever the
judge said, to protest by whatever means possible at the expensive
charade.

But though we now had just one charge active against each of
us, defending our position under Section 2 was not easy. John
Berry had the hardest job of all. He had actually signed forms
reminding him of the law many times, and had known the risk
he was taking. It was therefore difficult for his barrister to argue
legally against his technical guilt. In the end, rather than give
evidence from the witness box, he made a statement from the
dock.

This half-hour speech turned out to be a powerful explanation of his personal and political views. He went through the reasoning that had led him to give us an interview in the first place, and emphasized that there was no question of financial or other pressures to make him speak. 'I was not and never have been a member of any organization which would have an interest in my making any disclosures,' he said. 'There was no question of my being used by anybody. The decision I took was a deeply personal one and was made over a period of months rather than minutes.' What he had done was the result of a conviction that too much secrecy, far from protecting the public interest, actually harmed it. 'The information we discussed may be official, some of it may be classified,' he concluded, 'but nobody can classify my mind.'

With Duncan and myself there were far greater legal problems for the prosecution. They had to prove that we knew we were breaking the law. So for almost six days Duncan was taken through every aspect of the interview, why he had asked certain questions, what his interest was in Sigint and what he had thought before going to see John Berry. In response he explained his concern about the cost, effectiveness and potential abuses of the gigantic eavesdropping network. He also said that he had considered the law, treated it in a common-sense way and even had with him at the time a copy of a statement from the government that the 'mere receipt of official information' would no longer be an offence. What was our interview, if it wasn't mere receipt?

My own session in the witness box was comparatively short, less than two days of questioning about how and why the interview had happened. To be asked to justify doing what was a regular part of my job – talking to people – was strange enough, but when I was questioned on what I knew of the law beforehand, I said quite honestly that never in my wildest dreams had I considered a journalistic interview to be covered by the Official Secrets Act.

Though both of us had intended to call several well-known journalists as specialist witnesses, this possibility was quickly excluded. Two national newspaper journalists did have the opportunity to support Duncan by saying they would also interview people covered by the Act – and decide what to publish on legal advice afterwards. This was exactly the issue: that we had never been given the chance to come to that decision. But having reluctantly heard their statements, the judge decided that what other people would do in the same situation wasn't relevant.

After several days of summing-up speeches, it was again the judge, who was becoming impatient with these lengthy and troublesome proceedings, who had the final word. On Duncan and myself, he said it was a matter of our honesty. Could we be believed in our explanations that we didn't think we were breaking the law? Why, for instance, had we gone separately to John Berry's flat? – a coincidence he clearly found suspicious. But on Berry himself, he had no doubt about the strength of the law. He firmly directed the jury to find him guilty, and after retiring for an hour they did exactly that. Though according to the law a jury has the right to go against a judge's direction, in practice they were given little choice.

There were then only two charges left for the twelve members of the jury to consider. But just as the trial itself had proved a marathon, so its concluding moments developed into a nail-biting drama. For hour after hour, in the privacy of their room, the jury turned over the arguments. Occasionally they returned to the court to ask questions, and from these it was clear that their concern was with the current status of the Official Secrets Act. They were particularly interested in the government's statement about 'mere receipt' no longer being a crime.

But whatever doubts certain members of the jury might have had, they were not easily resolved. The hours soon turned into days, and for two successive nights the jury was confined to a special hotel, closely watched by court officials. During the day we waited nervously in the Old Bailey cafeteria, ears pricked for any announcement over the internal 'tannoy' system which might signal some activity in court. Every so often, the judge would recall the jury to ask them if they had reached some verdict. They hadn't.

Eventually they returned to court for the ninth time and announced they *had* reached a verdict. Duncan Campbell was guilty. But they had still not made up their minds about my case. They had also, according to the jury foreman, no prospect of reaching a decision.

For another day and a night the jury considered my position alone. The following morning the judge told them that unless at least ten of them (a majority) could agree, 'this man will have to stand trial before another jury'. Within an hour they returned with their third verdict: I was guilty as well. What the jury didn't realize was that the prosecution had already decided that the last thing they wanted was another ABC case. If the jury had been 'hung', we would therefore never have stood trial again.

Our sentences were about as mild as we could ever have expected. Against a maximum sentence of two years in prison under Section 2, John Berry was given a suspended sentence of six months. Duncan and myself received conditional discharges, the equivalent of a rap over the knuckles. We were, however, ordered to pay a total of £5,000 towards the prosecution costs. The only word of rebuke from the judge was to John. 'We will not tolerate defectors or whistleblowers from our services who seek the assistance of the press,' he said. 'In future they will go to prison.'

To the outside world the greatest surprise was that none of us actually *had* gone to prison. After a trial lasting on and off for two and a half months, a cost to the taxpayer of an estimated £250,000, it had ended in a whimper, not a bang. In a leading article the *Observer* said that 'the government's hamfisted attempts to silence radical journalists on the subject of electronic intelligence have ended with almost nothing salvaged from the wreckage ... After the pompous declarations of endangered national security which began the trial more than two months ago, it was a feeble anti-climax to a disastrous sequence of mistakes.'[1] The *Guardian* was equally forthright, describing the trial as 'an abuse of the legal process for which the three defendants should be entitled to redress. It has been the cause of serious doubt about the judgement and direction of the security services.'[2] The most common descriptions in the press were

1. *Observer*, 19.11.78.
2. *Guardian*, 18.11.78.

'farcical' and 'ludicrous', and there were calls for the immediate
resignation of Sam Silkin.

But as we sipped champagne and celebrated our freedom, the
final surprise came yet again from the jury. That evening four of
its members arrived at the pub where we were celebrating to
explain how they had come to their decision. They revealed that
during their exceptionally long retirement they had started, in
both my own and Duncan's cases, with a majority for 'not
guilty'. They had even considered going against the judge's
direction on John Berry. What had brought them round was not
the issue of our honesty but the sheer strength of the law. The
foreman in particular, unlike his military predecessor, had
strong moral reservations about what they had done. That the
jury members who had convicted us should have come to, in
effect, apologize for their action was the final extraordinary
feature of an extraordinary trial.

Conclusion

Looking back, my memory of those climactic two months spent sitting in the dock of Number 1 Court at the Old Bailey is a mixture of heightened nervousness and subdued farce: nervousness because we never *knew*, however confident we might have felt on occasion, that we could succeed in breaking through the barrier of security; subdued farce because, despite the outrageous nature of the incidents which frequently interrupted the smooth running of the proceedings, they were always translated into the cold language of the legal profession, anaesthetized of all emotion. At one point, the ABC Campaign even entered into this bizarre spirit by sending the first trial judge, Mr Justice Willis, a bunch of six red roses at the hospital where he was recuperating. He wrote back courteously thanking us for our consideration.

In describing the ABC trial, I have underlined its more dramatic moments but added little comment. It is important that I now make it clear that the seeds of the trial's failure were sown at the very point of our arrest and in the practices of the security system I have described. On the one hand, the secret world, spearheaded by the bureaucrats at Government Communications Headquarters, could see only that our interview covered totally forbidden territory and that they must therefore push our prosecution to its limit. This restricted vision, by its very nature, obscured their real potential for succeeding in court. On the other hand, they genuinely expected, as they said to journalist Gerry Gable, that the 'decent people' who were initially shocked at our arrest would evaporate, a process they were prepared to encourage. Instead, the benefits of our continuing public campaign reached their peak at the very point when they were needed most.

When those two elements – the exaggeration of the secrets

themselves and the strength of public outrage – came together, as they did during the trial, there was no escaping its ignominious collapse. As the *Daily Telegraph* said in opening its post-mortem on the day after our sentences: 'The ABC secrets trial had all the ingredients, including mystery and intrigue, of a major spy trial, but one vital element was missing – the spies.'

Who was to blame for that incredible waste of public time and money? Of the politicians, Sam Silkin, the Attorney-General, played a central role, giving government sanction to our prosecution under increasingly serious charges. He had to determine the validity of the security services' grave warnings, but failed to perceive their true character. He also approved the disastrous prosecution of the Colonel B contempt case. Silkin himself has always maintained that he thought long and hard about whether to proceed, studying the evidence and delaying a decision, and still has no doubt that his conclusion was correct. But it is interesting to note that after the trial, he described our campaign as 'unprecedented in my experience', and that he has since been replaced as the Labour spokesman on legal matters.

Merlyn Rees, then Home Secretary, should also not escape some blame. He not only approved the Agee–Hosenball deportations, but he was also responsible at that time for the Security Service, MI5, for general policy on the police and for phone-tapping and letter-opening. He must therefore have been in a position to make himself aware of at least some of what was happening behind the scenes in terms of investigations and snooping. David Owen, then Foreign Secretary and technically in charge of GCHQ, was in a similar position.

It is too easy, however, to criticize only the politicians, simply because they are publicly identifiable. The real onus of responsibility for the ABC case rests on the organizations of the secret world, whom nobody elected. The dangers of their isolation, independence and power remain the principal lessons to be learned from our prosecution.

In fact the ABC case raised a number of important issues, from jury vetting to the law of contempt, but did it actually affect the thinking of the decision-makers? On the legal side, the

Official Secrets Act is still, at the time of writing, the law of the land, and the influence of our case on government thinking would seem to have been negative rather than positive. Proposals for the reform of Section 2 of the law, put forward by the Conservative government in October 1979, would have strengthened it in the areas of security, defence and the police, whilst excluding from prosecution only the more mundane revelations. It would also have made information on defence and international relations protected, whether officially classified or not; it would have allowed a Ministerial certificate to be presented in court as conclusive evidence that information was secret; and – a direct reflection of the ABC trial – it would have made impossible a defence, such as ours, that information in the most sensitive areas was previously published.

Fortunately those proposals died a death, partly because of the hostility of the entire national press, partly because of the coincidence of the Anthony Blunt scandal. If the Tory Bill had become law, it was pointed out, Blunt might never have been unmasked. It is also true that if Blunt had been brought to trial, as many people thought he should, he would have faced charges under Section 1 of the Official Secrets Act. As James Callaghan, Prime Minister during the ABC case, said – perhaps unwittingly – during the uproar over the Blunt affair: 'I wonder if the same treatment would have been given to a humble corporal.' The double standard of the security services, and the real purpose of the law in prosecuting internal dissidents rather than spies, were clearly underlined. It remains to be seen whether the continuing pressure for more open government will lead to a genuine reform of the Act.

But the Blunt affair also raised other issues, in particular the accountability of the security services to parliament. To what extent, for instance, were even Ministers aware that this crucial figure in the penetration of British security by the Russians had been granted immunity from prosecution? This added fuel to the second major element of the ABC case – the vital question of whether the secrecy surrounding the operations of the agencies of national security can be justified.

With this there has been little progress, though two small

examples are worthy of note. On telephone-tapping and letter-opening, the government has been forced to publish its first report since that of the Birkett Committee in 1957, though a decidedly meagre eight-page effort. At the same time, it also made the system subject to regular review by a judge, though again this falls short of the standards expected by the European Court of Human Rights – and tapping still has no legal basis. On jury vetting, a revised version of Sam Silkin's guidelines was issued by his Conservative successor, Michael Havers, in 1980 – a response to what he called 'keen public interest'. This merely tinkered with the system, however, limiting Special Branch checks to terrorist and 'national security' trials where *in camera* evidence is heard. It would not stop vetting in a trial such as ours.

But it would be wrong to see the influence of the ABC case entirely in terms of direct parliamentary or legal action. The wheels of government grind slowly, and a major event can lodge itself in the political subconscious, adding weight to a change of mind which only later emerges as an apparently quite independent initiative. Governments of all complexions dislike intensely being prompted into action by their own mistakes.

The most important effect of our case, and the deportation of Agee and Hosenball before it, has in fact been a growing awareness among people outside government of the apparatus which exists, its uses and its potential abuses. In numerous small ways, individuals who became involved in the ABC campaign or who just read about it have taken the issue of national security much closer to the centre of their political consciousness.

Examples of this include the development of State Research, a group which monitors and publishes information on security, and the Labour Party's recent decision to circulate its members asking for their views on the security services. At the same time, there have been the renewed investigations of my co-defendant Duncan Campbell into such areas as phone-tapping. The decision by the former Sigint officer, Jock Kane, to push his concern into the public limelight (see Chapter 5) was also directly the result of his anger at the ABC trial. I hope this book will have widened that interest still further. For, in an area so smothered by red tape, it is only by knowing more about what is going on that individuals can formulate their own ideas.

If that process continues, what changes can we hope for over the next ten years? To start with, the Official Secrets Act requires total replacement, not just by a mild reform of Section 2 but by a genuine Freedom of Information Act along the lines already in operation in the United States. This would reverse the situation where everything is automatically protected and would place the burden on the government to justify withholding information. In Canada, which has a constitution modelled on the British one and an Official Secrets Act, just such a proposal has been suggested by the government, giving the lie to the argument that it is unsuitable here. But alongside that there needs to be much closer monitoring of the security services, so that parliament as a whole can oversee the direction of their policies and activities. The system of permanent intelligence committees established in America provides the model for this.

As far as the information collected by the agencies is concerned, there should be a legal right of access, either by members of the public or by a body acting on their behalf, to ensure that the files are both accurate and are kept for purposes which are acceptable to the people. Precedents for this can be found on the statute books of Sweden and Austria, for example. Britain remains one of the few European countries not to have implemented even a data protection law – or any legislation guaranteeing its citizens' privacy – though it may soon be forced to by the European Convention on Human Rights.

Finally, we need a change in the political climate which will make these reforms possible. Given the revelations of the past few years, of which the ABC case is just one example, it is no longer reasonable for us to sit back and imagine that our intelligence and security services operate with the same gentlemanly integrity of which wartime histories are made. If the politicians refuse to budge, then investigators, journalists and pressure groups will have to push them. The possibility that even more 'secrets' will emerge from such inquiries should not frighten those who fear for our democratic traditions. To place the agencies of national security firmly within the context of democracy would strengthen rather than weaken our social fabric.

In 1983 the Special Branch will be exactly a century old, only just before we reach the doomsday year of George Orwell's nightmare. We are not as close to that society as some pessimists have suggested. But only if the dangers which can result from some of the activities I have described are recognized will we be certain to avoid the fulfilment of that vision.

Appendix: Chronology of main events surrounding the ABC case

21 May 1976

The 'Eavesdroppers' article by Mark Hosenball and Duncan Campbell, about Signals Intelligence, published in *Time Out*.

30 June 1976

Winslow Peck, former American signals analyst quoted in the 'Eavesdroppers' article, refused entry to Britain.

16 November 1976

American writers Philip Agee and Mark Hosenball served with deportation orders for reasons of 'national security'.

January 1977

Agee and Hosenball appear before three Home Office-appointed advisers to review their cases. 'The Eavesdroppers' suspected to be the real reason for Hosenball's expulsion.

January–February 1977

Suspected surveillance of the Agee–Hosenball Defence Committee.

4 February 1977

John Berry writes a letter to the Agee–Hosenball Defence Committee.

16 February 1977

Home Secretary Merlyn Rees confirms the deportations.

18 February 1977

Crispin Aubrey and Duncan Campbell interview Berry. All three arrested and charged under Section 2 of the Official Secrets Act.

24 May 1977

Attorney-General Sam Silkin approves the prosecution. Further charges added under Setion 1, the 'spying' clause.

9 August 1977

Additional charge against Duncan Campbell of 'collecting information', also under Section 1.

18 November 1977

Aubrey, Berry and Campbell committed to the Old Bailey for trial. Colonel B appears as main prosecution witness. Protests at his anonymity.

December 1977–January 1978

Colonel B named as Colonel H. A. Johnstone in two magazines, *Peace News* and the *Leveller*, and later in the *Journalist*, newspaper of the National Union of Journalists.

20 April 1978

Colonel B identified by four MPs in the House of Commons, his name broadcast on TV and printed in the national press.

May 1978

High Court action by the Attorney-General against the three publications which originally named the Colonel. Lord Justice Widgery imposes fines totalling £1,200.

5 September 1978

ABC trial opens at the Old Bailey.

18 September 1978

Trial stopped by Russell Harty TV programme report on jury member's background as Special Air Services officer.

3 October 1978

Second trial opens. Separate charge against Duncan Campbell dropped.

24 October 1978

All Section 1 charges dropped after the judge describes them as 'oppressive'.

17 November 1978

Trial ends. Aubrey, Berry and Campbell receive minor, non-custodial sentences under Section 2, a part of the law the government is committed to repeal.

February 1979

House of Lords overturns High Court judgment on the naming of Colonel B. Fines and costs are repaid to the three magazines.

Select Bibliography

1. Books

Ackroyd, Carol, Karen Margolis, Jonathan Rosenhead, and Tim Shallice, *The Technology of Political Control* (Penguin, 1977).

Agee, Philip, *Inside The Company : CIA Diary* (Penguin, 1975).

Agee, Philip and Louis Wolf, (eds), *Dirty Work : The CIA in Western Europe* (Lyle Stuart, 1978).

Aitken, Jonathan, *Officially Secret* (Weidenfeld and Nicolson, 1971).

Bulloch, John, *MI5* (Barker, 1963).

Bunyan, Tony, *The Political Police in Britain* (Julian Friedmann, 1976).

Halperin, Morton, Jerry Berman, Robert Borosage, and Christine Marwick, *The Lawless State : The Crimes of the US Intelligence Agencies* (Penguin USA, 1976).

Hewitt, Patricia, *Privacy : The Information Gatherers* (NCCL, 1977).

Kahn, David, *The Codebreakers* (Sphere, 1973).

Marchetti, Victor and John Marks, *The CIA and the Cult of Intelligence* (Coronet, 1976).

O'Higgins, Paul, *Censorship in Britain* (Nelson, 1972).

Pincher, Chapman, *Inside Story* (Sidgwick and Jackson, 1978).

Robertson, Geoff, *Reluctant Judas* (Temple Smith, 1976).

Thompson, Anthony, *Big Brother in Britain Today* (Michael Joseph, 1970).

Thompson, Edward, *Writing by Candlelight* (Merlin Press, 1980).

Williams, David, *Not in the Public Interest* (Hutchinson, 1972).

Wise, David and Thomas Ross, *The Intelligence Establishment* (Jonathan Cape, 1968).

2. Official Reports and Proposed Legislation

Report of the Committee of Privy Councillors Appointed to Inquire into the Interception of Communications : The Birkett Report (Cmnd 283, HMSO 1957).

Security Procedures in the Public Service : The Radcliffe Report (Cmnd 1681, HMSO 1962).

Lord Denning's Report (Cmnd 2152, HMSO 1963).

Departmental Committee on Section 2 of the Official Secrets Act, 1911:
The Franks Report (Cmnd 5104, HMSO 1972).

Report of the Committee on Privacy: The Younger Report (Cmnd 5012, HMSO 1972).

United States Senate Select Committee to Study Governmental Operations with Respect to Intelligence Activities: The Church Report (United States Government Printing Office, 1975–6).

United States House of Representatives Select Committee on Intelligence: extracts reprinted as *CIA: The Pike Report* (Spokesman Books, 1977).

Report of the Committee on Data Protection: The Lindop Report (Cmnd 7341, HMSO 1978).

Reform of Section 2 of the Official Secrets Act, 1911: Labour Government White Paper (Cmnd 7285, HMSO 1978).

Official Information Bill: Private Member's Bill 'to create a public right of access to official information' (HMSO 1978).

Disclosure of Official Information: A Report on Overseas Practice (HMSO 1979).

Protection of Official Information Bill: Conservative Government proposal (HMSO 1979).

The Interception of Communications in Great Britain (Cmnd 7873, HMSO 1980).

3. Pamphlets

Open Up! (Fabian Society, 1980). Fabian pamphlet on freedom of information.

The State Versus Its 'Enemies' by E. P. Thompson (Merlin Press, 1979).

The Right to Know by Tony Benn (Institute for Workers' Control, 1978).

The Politics of Secrecy: The Case for a Freedom of Information Law by James Michael (NCCL, 1979).

Justice Deserted: The Subversion of the Jury by Harriet Harman and John Griffith (NCCL, 1979).

Tapping the Telephone (Post Office Engineering Union, 1980).

4. Useful Organizations

State Research, 9 Poland Street, London W1.
　　Publishes regular bulletins and pamphlets.

National Council for Civil Liberties, 182 Kings Cross Road, London WC1.
　　Watchdog body, publishes reports.

Covert Action Information Bulletin, PO Box 50272, Washington DC 20004.

   Monitors US intelligence activities.

Center for National Security Studies, 122 Maryland Avenue NE, Washington DC 20002.

   Publishes a regular bulletin on US spying, *First Principles: National Security and Civil Liberties.*

Index

More About Penguins and Pelicans